Mediterranean Diet for Beginners

The Ultimate Step-by-Step Healthy Guide to Lose Up to 12 Pounds in 4 Weeks, with Easy, Affordable, Delicious Recipes

By
Sasha Taylor

Respective authors own all copyrights not held by the publisher.

The information herein is offered for informational purposes solely and is universal as so.

The presentation of the information is without a contract or any guarantee assurance.

The trademarks that are used are without any consent, and the publication of the trademark is without permission or backing by the trademark owner. All trademarks and brands within this book are for clarifying purposes only and are owned by the owners themselves, not affiliated with this document.

TABLE OF CONTENTS

INTRODUCTION

The Mediterranean Diet is known as a type of diet that is created from healthy habits which combine physical exercises with an eating pattern that has multiple health benefits. This diet was created based on the consumption habits of the Mediterranean Sea populations, hence its name. It is characterized as being one of the healthiest and most balanced diets because it includes a wide variety of foods that offer different fresh products in specific seasons.

Rather than being a diet, they are habits that can be maintained as time goes by, thus maintaining it as a lifestyle. One of the great benefits offered by this diet is the ability to reduce the risk of developing cardiovascular diseases such as heart attacks and strokes. In addition to helping to lose weight, it also lowers blood pressure and blood glucose levels, and prevents alterations that influence risk factors to the heart. In addition to this, its great contribution to the best gastrointestinal functioning also includes a large amount of vitamins and antioxidants from its foods that help prevent diseases and viruses, retarding the aging process.

The foods allowed in this diet include vegetables, dried and fresh fruits, fish, poultry, whole grains, skim milk, yogurt, and olive oil. Both eggs and red meat are recommended from time to time. Fresh raw food is the main attraction of this diet and its main cooking methods are grilled and oven. Salads are also common dishes, and desserts should be based on mixed fruits. Natural dressings are also important in this eating habit since garlic and onions are key to flavor naturally, as are fresh herbs such as parsley, oregano, and basil.

As for liquids, water and wine are the most ingested. However, coffee and tea can be consumed in very small quantities. The foods that should be avoided when practicing this diet are the excesses of red meat and processed foods, as well as frozen and canned foods that contain chemicals. Sweetbreads, refined flour, sugary drinks, and non-olive oils should also be avoided.

CHAPTER 1

THE BENEFITS OF THE MEDITERRANEAN DIET

This year, on the 16th of October, World Food Day is celebrated. Its purpose is to strengthen solidarity in the fight against hunger, malnutrition, and poverty. Likewise, it also aims to raise public awareness about the food problems that exist in the world.

In this sense, a balanced diet helps us feel better about ourselves, stronger and healthier, and lead a more orderly and satisfying life in many aspects. Thus, one of the Spanish diets, the Mediterranean Diet, is one of the most complete that exist, and that in turn brings numerous benefits to our health. Fresh products, fruits, and vegetables, or legumes and vegetables make up this diet that is so nutritious and recommended.

What is the Mediterranean Diet?

UNESCO registers the Mediterranean Diet as one of the elements of the "Representative List of the Intangible Cultural Heritage of Humanity." This diet is closely linked to the food pyramid, which makes it the healthiest regimen for us. The bases of a correct Mediterranean Diet are:

- **Use olive oil:** we have already talked about the virtues of liquid gold and its advantages over other fats. It is rich in vitamins and monounsaturated fatty acids, so, unlike other types of oils or butter, it takes care of our body and our cardiovascular health.

- **Eat plant foods such as fruits, vegetables, or mushrooms:** a source of vitamins and fiber that provide a large amount of water. They are natural antioxidants, and consuming them helps us prevent certain types of diseases.
- **Nuts:** a handful of almonds gives us calcium, phosphorus and magnesium, and multiple vitamins Group B. But it is not advisable to abuse them.
- Bread and other foods from cereals such as pasta or rice are necessary due to their contribution as carbohydrates, needed to provide power during the day. It is best not to eat them for dinner since they have a great caloric intake.
- **Eat more fish than red meat.** In the Mediterranean Diet, it is recommended to consume fish twice a week, at a minimum. Meats, better lean, in small quantities.
- **Eggs contain very good quality proteins and many vitamins.** Eating between three and four eggs per week is ideal since they also have a lot of cholesterol.

Try to always choose fresh and seasonal foods.

Water consumption is vital for our body, and the Mediterranean diet recommends between 1.5 and

2 liters of water a day to stay hydrated inside and out.

To follow this regime appropriately, processed meat (such as sausages), sugars, pastries and cakes, concentrated and sugary juices, soft drinks, and sweets should be dispensed as far as possible.

What are the benefits of the Mediterranean Diet?

This lifestyle helps us take care of ourselves both inside and out. With the consumption of fresh and vegetable foods, our skin will remain younger thanks to the antioxidants in food, as well as our cells. The necessary water supply helps to hydrate our skin and eradicate problems such as cellulite or fluid retention. Also, this diet is ideal to end overweight and obesity.

On the other hand, the multiple properties of these foods keep our hearts healthy and our allies in the fight against diabetes and Alzheimer's. Some diseases, such as breast or colon cancer, can be prevented with the proper application of this diet.

Many scientific studies have examined the effects of the Mediterranean Diet. One of the most recent, undertaken by the Mediterranean Neurological Institute's (Neuromed) Department of Epidemiology and Prevention, suggests that it is a good food choice for those over 65 because it leads to healthier aging. So the main advantages of the Mediterranean diet are:

The Mediterranean diet helps maintain heart health

Many of the foods which make up the Mediterranean lifestyle are cardioprotective. Research published in the European Journal of Heart Failure points out that the Mediterranean diet reduces the risk of heart failure by 31 percent. Foods like olive oil and nuts help to lower cholesterol levels, as they are rich sources of monounsaturated fatty acids. Their omega-three and omega-6 content also help to improve cardiovascular health.

Prevents obesity and overweight

All nuts and olive oil do not get fat as long as we take them slowly. Quite the reverse; they help us to prevent problems such as overweight and obesity because, according to the Primed study, those who follow a Mediterranean diet manage to lose weight and improve their health.

Also, according to the authors of this work, the consumption of nuts could help you lose weight in hypocaloric diets. One explanation for this is the satiety effect they create, with adequate amounts and guidance.

The Mediterranean diet helps regulate intestinal transit

A sufficient amount of fruit and vegetables, at least 400 grams per day, minus potatoes and other tubers, tend to control intestinal movement and avoid constipation from a sporadic occurrence. This is due to the daily input of dietary fiber and whole-grain consumption, which is very beneficial to normal digestive system functioning.

A Mediterranean diet with antioxidant effect

Some of the Mediterranean diet's traditional fruits and vegetables, including pomegranate or carrot, are abundant in antioxidants—such as beta-carotene—that protect the body against free radicals, causing various health problems.

It favors the quality of life

The Mediterranean lifestyle consists of good habits, such as taking the opportunity to relax or a 15-20 minute nap, which can have a positive effect on the quality of life, as we prefer relaxation and disconnection in difficult conditions.

The Mediterranean diet, which we ought to be proud of, is a way of understanding food and culture, using new and local ingredients, enjoying nature, and maintaining traditional traditions that do not harm our health.

CHAPTER 2

DIETS THAT COMPETE WITH THE TRADITIONAL MEDITERRANEAN DIET

The traditional Mediterranean diet, however, is not the only reference for healthy eating patterns. Below we discover other diets that have nothing to envy.

We are going to present in this chapter five diets that have turned out to be as healthy as the traditional Mediterranean diet. Let us know their characteristics and health benefits. They are:

- Nordic diet
- Paleo
- Japanese diet
- Vegetarian
- The Harvard dish

Nordic diet

The World Health Organization (WHO) recently highlighted the advantages of the Scandinavian diet as a healthy eating style. The positive effects are aimed at reducing the risk of non-communicable diseases such as cancer, diabetes, or other cardiovascular problems.

This diet is focused on foods originating from northern European countries: Iceland, Sweden, Finland, Norway, and Denmark. A group of chefs from these northern countries came together to develop the so-called New Nordic Diet beginning in 2004.

Its objective is to promote the consumption of local, wild, and fresh ingredients to enhance health, gastronomy, sustainability, and Nordic identity. And what are these foods? Basically:

- Fruits and berries.
- Rapeseed oil.
- Whole grains (rye, barley, and oats) and legumes.
- Vegetable greens.
- Fatty fish (herring, mackerel, or salmon) several times a week.
- Low-fat dairy.

A paleo diet

It is increasingly common to hear about this diet. Although little by little it is becoming popular in our country, this is the traditional diet of some groups that live in the Amazon rainforest, in the African savanna or certain Pacific islands.

In the paleo, or paleolithic diet, we propose a way to feed ourselves according to our genetics and evolution as a species. It is based on eating in a similar way to how our hunter ancestors did. This diet includes:

- Vegetables

- Seeds and nuts
- Fish and seafood
- Meat and offal
- Eggs
- Fruits

In turn, dairy products, gluten, and grains are completely neglected. Medical studies have shown good results in:

- Reduction of coronary risk.
- Reduction in indicators of inflammation.
- Greater loss of abdominal circumference.

Japanese diet

The Okinawa Islands are located in southern Japan. They stand out on the world map not only because of the elegance of their environments but also because they are the world's region with the longest-lived and improved health.

Among the many reasons for this longevity, their diet stands out without any doubt. There are many scientists who have studied it, although studies are lacking to assess the effects it can have on non-Japanese people. Perhaps this is the greatest difference between the Japanese and the Mediterranean or the Nordic diet.

The daily menu of the Japanese do not lack:

- Leafy green vegetables.

- A couple of days a week with fish and cephalopods, such as squid or octopus.
- Soy and its derivatives like tofu. Cereals integrals and sweet potatoes.
- kombu.

Another signature feature of the Japanese diet is that they consume food several times a day in small amounts and with a wide variety of ingredients included in each meal.

Vegetarian diet

The International Vegetarian Union describes the vegetarian diet as "a diet focused on plant-derived ingredients, with or without dairy products, eggs and/or honey."

This aspect makes it a food pattern that can vary a bit between vegans, ovo-vegetarians, ovo-dairy vegetarians, etc., but which is mostly based on plant-based foods. The result is a considerable contribution of foods rich in vitamins, minerals, fiber, and low in cholesterol and saturated fats.

Among the benefits of this type of diet, we can see good results in:

- Reduction of the risk of suffering from hypertension.
- Hypercholesterolaemia.
- Heart problems.

'Harvard dish' method

A healthy eating dish is a tool created by nutrition experts from the Harvard School of Public Health. It aims to be a guide to help the American population make better choices in relation to their diet.

It is a very visual tool that recommends filling half the plate with fruits and vegetables, a room with some source of protein, and another room with sources of carbohydrates.

In addition, it also focuses on the quality of the diet and not only on the amounts. It recommends, for example, consuming whole grains instead of refined flours, drinking water instead of soda or energy drinks, and not making low-fat diets but choosing good vegetable oils and nuts.

What happens then with the traditional Mediterranean diet?

All the diets we have analyzed have proven to be healthy ways of eating. As we have seen, they all have points in common with the traditional Mediterranean diet:

- They are based on the consumption of fresh and local products, rich in fiber, vitamins, minerals, and phytochemicals.
- They also have good sources of protein and healthy fats.

- There is no consumption of prepared foods, rich in sugars and refined flours, or large amounts of red meat or saturated fat recommended.

Therefore, we can conclude that in the countries of the Mediterranean basin, the traditional Mediterranean diet is the best way to eat , although similar diets are perfectly valid at each site. It must be a well-planned diet, adapted to the needs of each individual and based on fresh and local foods, such as olive oil, sardines, nuts, or chickpeas.

We must never forget that a diet, in order to work, must always be accompanied by healthy living habits; do not abandon them!

CHAPTER 3

THE MEDITERRANEAN DIET CAN RELIEVE CHRONIC PAIN IN OBESITY

Research suggests that eating fish and vegetable proteins reduces inflammation in obese patients. People with obesity can therefore benefit from the Mediterranean diet to prevent or alleviate chronic pain.

Research into obesity

The study was conducted among 98 men and women between 20 and 78 years old. It builds on earlier results that a diet rich in fish, fruit, vegetables, nuts and beans have significant health benefits. In addition, it sheds new light on the beneficial effects of the diet to relieve chronic pain in obesity.

Because obesity patients generally have more inflammation, the anti-inflammatory effect of the diet can reduce pain. Although the relationship between body fat and pain has been well documented in previous studies, the mechanism behind it is still unknown. One possible cause is the pressure that body weight exerts on joints. Another possible mechanism works through the bloodstream, because both body fat and pain are associated with increased inflammation.

The method

For the study, the eating habits of the participants were assessed and they had to answer questions about the pain they experienced. The age, mental health and medication use of the participants were included in the results. Regardless of body weight and gender, participants with a Mediterranean diet were found to experience less pain.

Limitations

The research does have limitations; they have not taken into account chronic pain that lasted longer than a month. In addition, no blood was taken to test for inflammation. More research is therefore needed to prove a causal relationship, because there is now only a relationship between the two factors. The next step is a test in which blood is tested for inflammation. Then it would be ideal to conduct an intervention study to evaluate changes in body fat, inflammation and pain levels.

A nutritionist who has assessed the study believes it emphasizes the health benefits of the Mediterranean diet. "The research provides an early look at the possible role that diet can play in compensating for pain," says Connie Diekman of Washington University. According to Diekman, however, more research is needed: "Research into healthy adults is needed to see if the same inflammatory values produce the same pain levels as in obese people."

In addition, future investigations must also be conducted over a longer period. According to Diekman, it is advantageous to know whether the Mediterranean diet at a young age causes less pain as the person ages.

Still, the new findings help to realize that what you eat is important. "It is an interesting study that gives us food for thought in assisting obesity patients. A diet can help the pain, but we don't have a clear answer yet if it will help you lose weight. More research is needed to find out.

CHAPTER 4

THE TOP HABITS TO MAKE A MEDITERRANEAN DIET

We tell you what the bases of the Mediterranean diet are so you can start carrying them out.

The Mediterranean diet is world-renowned. It is definitely one of the healthiest diets in the world and has, on several occasions, consistently reached the top of the rankings. Today we want to share the top ten habits for a Mediterranean diet with you.

Continue reading and discover in this chapter the main tips to carry out this balanced diet every day in your home. You will not regret it!

Top 10 habits for the Mediterranean diet

If you want to change eating habits and resume your diet in the Mediterranean, get a paper and pencil, and take notes. Below we will present the 10 bases of this cultural heritage:

1. Olive oil as a base fat

Olive oil is the fat that is most found everywhere you look. Rich in antioxidants, monounsaturated, and vitamin E fatty acids, from dressing salads to frying, it is used for everything.

Are you preparing toast? Do not hesitate: a dash of olive oil may be the touch you need. Do you plan to fry some potatoes? Or are you preparing a salad? Undoubtedly, olive oil is used over any other type of oil and even over butter.

2. Fresh food every day!

The Mediterranean diet is based on new and seasonal food consumption. That is, each season, you will buy some fruits and vegetables. In this way, you can profit from all its nutritional value and save money! If you also pick local food, make sure that you buy the best quality at the best price.

3. Steps to make a Mediterranean diet: Fruits and vegetables at each meal

This indication goes hand in hand with the preceding point for making the Mediterranean diet. Include fruits and vegetables in each meal. You will eat 1 to 2 pieces of fruit a day, and about 3 servings of vegetables a day. How can you do it? Let's look at several examples:

- Breakfast: toast with tomato and olive oil, and a piece of fruit.
- Eat nuts in the middle of the morning.
- Have some pasta with sautéed vegetables and for dessert, fruit.
- Snack on a yogurt with fruits or nuts, or a sandwich with avocado and ham.
- Eat baked fish with salad and potatoes. For dessert: fruit.

4. Fish several times a week

Reduce red meat consumption and emphasis on improving seafood consumption. You should eat white and bluefish at least twice a week. The options are multiple: baked, grilled, fried, sautéed... Its contribution to Omega-3 fatty acids will help you maintain vascular health by reducing cholesterol and blood triglycerides.

5. Eggs, four times a week

Contrary to what you may believe, eggs are healthy. Years and studies have passed since the time when the egg was believed to be harmful to health. We know today that the egg is a source of high-quality proteins, vitamins, and monounsaturated and polyunsaturated fats.

The egg problem is the conviction that it increases cholesterol. This is not so, though. At least not completely: excess egg consumption, along with other factors such as sedentary lifestyle and stress, could trigger cholesterol values. Of course, fried, cooked or boiled is always better to eat.

6. Steps for a Mediterranean diet: Regular consumption of dairy products

In the Mediterranean diet, cheeses and yogurts are part of daily meals. This is because they are rich in carbohydrates, nutrients like calcium or phosphorus, and high biologically important proteins. An idea, anyway? You may add a slice of fruit cheese, or even yogurt, with fruit pieces inside. How about if the pieces of feta cheese are mixed with salad?

7. Minimizes the consumption of red meat

It is important to reduce the intake of red meat to make a Mediterranean diet, instead of choosing to eat white meat such as chicken and fish. Recall that the World Health Organization cautioned a few years ago of possible problems caused by excessive intake of processed and red meat.

8. Cereals every day

Cereals are part of the food pyramid foundation as they give us resources. Mainly, the choice of integral versions of pasta, rice, couscous, and bread is usually recommended.

9. Steps to make a Mediterranean diet: Minimum intake of sweets

Sweets, pastries, and goodies can be consumed extremely moderately. That is, its consumption is not prohibited, but it must be controlled in the extreme. Bear in mind that too much sugar can cause illnesses like diabetes or obesity. Less than two servings per week is perfect.

10. Water at all hours

The preferred drink should always be water: it quenches thirst and does not provide empty calories to the body. It is advised to moderate to the extreme the consumption of sugary drinks, such as soft drinks and industrial juices.

What do you think about making the Mediterranean diet out of this top ten? As you can see from this, it is not so difficult to follow. You just have to adapt your habits to eat healthy foods and minimize the consumption of the least healthy, in addition to regular physical exercise!

CHAPTER 5

WHAT CAN MOTIVE YOU TO FOLLOW THIS DIET

The Mediterranean diet is considered to be one of the dietary patterns with the strongest accumulated scientific evidence of its human health benefits.

Following the Mediterranean diet is one of the easiest options to maintain your ideal weight, and to take care of your health. But what is special about this diet? We invite you to continue reading and know all the benefits that this diet can bring to your health.

The Mediterranean diet is not just a series of nutritional recommendations; it is much more than that. It is associated with a balanced lifestyle and constitutes a true cultural heritage of the people of the Mediterranean basin.

Yes, it was proclaimed the Intangible Cultural Heritage of Humanity in a shared language of Spain, Greece, Italy, and Morocco on 16 November 2010.

What foods make up the Mediterranean diet?

The Mediterranean diet is characterized in that all kinds of food can be eaten, as long as the famous food pyramid is respected, which provides the basis of what foods should be taken daily, which ones should be taken weekly, and which should be taken occasionally.

Foods to eat daily:

Cereals: Pasta, rice, and bread are an example of this, so experts recommend taking 30 grams of bread daily, and between 60 and 80 grams of pasta and rice a day.

Fruit and vegetables: The base of the nutritional pyramid indicates that 5 pieces of fruit and vegetables (alternate) should be taken per day, which corresponds to 120-180 grams of fruit, and between 150 and 200 grams of vegetables.

Foods to ingest daily:

- A liter and a half of water daily
- A glass of milk or two yogurts
- A tablespoon of extra virgin olive oil raw
- Dressings such as onion and garlic also raw

Foods to eat weekly:

- Fish
- Lean meat
- Red meat: one serving per week is advised
- Eggs: two to four weekly servings
- Legumes and potatoes: advised 3 times per week

Foods that should be ingested occasionally:

- Pastries
- Candy
- Sugar
- Sugary juices and soft drinks

10 Reasons That Will Convince You To Follow The Mediterranean Diet

1. Considered one of the best diets in science

The Mediterranean diet is considered one of the dietary patterns with the highest accumulated evidence regarding its benefits in human health.

It has long been a focus of interest in the scientific community, especially for its therapeutic role against various pathologies associated with chronic inflammation, such as metabolic syndrome, diabetes, cardiovascular disease, neurodegenerative diseases, and cancer, among others.

2. Boosts good cholesterol

According to researchers from the Center for Biomedical Research in the Pathophysiology Network of Obesity and Nutrition (CIBEROBN) and the Hospital del Mar Institute for Medical Research (IMIM), The Mediterranean diet allows the particles containing so-called healthy cholesterol, which stop blocked arteries, to function properly.

3. Reduces the risk of cardiovascular diseases

Different studies have revealed that in Mediterranean countries, people suffer less cardiovascular disease than in other countries, due to the high amount of nutrients contained in traditional recipes.

4. Reduces the risk of breast cancer, heart attacks, and strokes

The Primed essay, headed by Miguel Ángel Martínez-González, Professor of Public Health at the University of Navarra and since June also a visiting professor at Harvard, has shown that the Mediterranean diet reduces circulation problems by 66%, heart attacks and strokes by 30% and the risk of breast cancer by 68%.

5. Fights severe depression

A team of scientists from the Australian University of Deakin conducted a series of tests that determined that the Mediterranean diet fights severe depression.

6. Increases longevity

Using the Mediterranean diet, people tend to live longer since it favors life expectancy and reduces the aging process thanks to its proposal to eat foods rich in antioxidants and high-quality nutrients.

7. Good for obesity

Several fats are used, and olive oil is the one used for cooking. Butter and other meat and vegetable fats typical of other diets are much safer than those. Thus it turns out to be a good option for dealing with obesity.

8. Avoids mental deterioration

Green leafy vegetables, which have many antioxidants, prevent cell degradation. Eating at least one serving per day of such vegetables helps slow cognitive decline associated with aging, as suggests a study published in the journal of Neurology.

9. Helps to achieve the ideal weight

The Mediterranean diet is very varied and with low caloric intake. If you combine it with physical exercise, you can get close to your ideal weight. Fighting against overweight also removes many diseases that worsen with physical fitness.

10. Following the Mediterranean diet helps the environment

One of the bases of the Mediterranean diet is the consumption of fresh and seasonal foods, so by adopting these eating habits you will be helping the environment by promoting an adequate use of its natural resources.

After reading these 10 reasons to follow the Mediterranean diet, have you not yet convinced yourself to try it out? Take advantage of the arrival of summer to benefit from the great variety of fruits and vegetables that the season gives us to start putting these tips in motion.

CHAPTER 6

MEDITERRANEAN DIET EXAMPLES

The Mediterranean diet excludes fats harmful to our bodies. It is focused on preserving those eating habits and a healthy diet.

It's true there are many different types of diet. Possibly too many. Yet experts tell us that we should look for those that are safer, those that provide us with the essential nutrients while helping us lose weight. The Mediterranean diet is rich in protein, carbohydrates, omega 3, whole grains, nutrients, vitamins, and, most notably, almost no processed oils, flours, and sugars.

Why is the Mediterranean diet able to help me lose weight?

First of all, we have to mention that the Mediterranean diet does not simply respond directly to a weight-loss process. It is about keeping very healthy eating habits where we are able to control our weight, due to its ingredients and behaviors, minus everything that can make us overweight or even get sick. Nutritionists tell us we can lose one kilogram a week with it.

By this, we mean the Mediterranean diet is beneficial not only to us but to the whole family as well. This fulfills the fundamental principles of the food pyramid proposed by the World Health Organization (WHO).

The Mediterranean diet benefits from its excellent contribution of healthy fats, olive oil, and only monounsaturated, and fatty acids such as Omega 6.

Animal protein is excluded, as well as red meat.

It is the diet rich in antioxidants: fruits, nuts, vegetables, and legumes...

Excellent fiber input.

We can reduce our blood cholesterol with the Mediterranean diet, shield ourselves from cardiovascular diseases, and take care of our weight thanks to this healthy source of nutrients where unhealthy fats are removed for our body.

What foods make up the Mediterranean diet?

- Vegetables, nuts, legumes, fruits like orange, lemon, melon, apples, grapes, etc.
- The primary source of fat is olive oil.
- Wine averaged in moderate amounts. Just one glass of it a day.
- Fish like tuna, salmon, or cod.
- Pasta as the main source of carbohydrates.

When eating meat, it is always either chicken or turkey. They're both lean meats.

Equally, beneficial lifestyle habits add to this balanced, varied, and healthy diet. Walking daily in the sun, thus absorbing the needed vitamin D, and the importance of breakfast and eating in a relaxed way, are habits we often miss because of our commitments, which are an integral part of our wellbeing.

Guidelines to meet the Mediterranean diet

You have to complete 5 meals a day, including breakfast, lunch, food, snacks and dinner. The aim is to eat small portions five times a day and never in large amounts.

Never go without food; it's important that you get the strength to start the day and support the entire day's commitment.

Dispense with the use of butter. Always replace it with olive oil.

- Dinners will be essentially vegetable-based.
- Do not exclude bread; it is essential to provide fiber. Choose those of whole grain; those of rye or oats are highly recommended.
- Highly recommended spices include: oregano, basil, parsley... And essential is garlic.
- Sweets are not permitted. Replace vegetable milk with cow's milk.

- Drinking a glass of wine a day is also recommended, as are two liters of water a day.

Mediterranean diet examples

Here are three menu examples. You can make the variations you want in the following days, knowing the foods are the healthiest in the Mediterranean diet. It is important that you always eat fruit and vegetables when they are fresh. If you feel hungry between hours, you can resort to nuts like pistachios. Seek new and organic fruit juices. Do not forget to sleep gently and exercise for at least one hour each day.

Menu 1

Breakfast:

- Orange juice, an integral toast with honey.

Lunch:

- An Apple.

Food:

- Lettuce salad, with half pomegranate and a splash of lemon.
- Baked breast with lemon.
- An infusion of green tea.

Snack

- A cup of grapes

Dinner

- Scrambled eggs with spinach and prawns.
- Baked hake.
- Apple juice.

Menu 2

Breakfast

- A cup of oatmeal with two nuts and a plum.

Lunch

- A skimmed yogurt.

Food

- Pasta salad with tomatoes, basil, black olives, and olive oil.
- Zucchini purée with oregano and pepper.

Snack

- A cup of apple jam.

Dinner

- Baked eggplants.
- A salad of lettuce and grated carrot.

- An infusion of chamomile and lemon balm.

Menu 3

Breakfast

- Oat milk and an apple.

Lunch

- An integral toast with natural tomato spread.

Food

- Brown rice with mushrooms.
- A salad of lettuce with two slices of orange.

Snack

- Peach juice.

Dinner

- Boiled artichokes with olive oil and a splash of vinegar.
- A spinach salad with turkey chips and pineapple chips.

CHAPTER 7

OLIVE OIL, THE BEST OF THE MEDITERRANEAN DIET

Although it can be used for cooking, it is recommended to take olive oil raw, such as in salad dressing or cold soups, since this would preserve all its properties.

It is a vegetable oil that is obtained from the olive or äliv (name in Latin), the fruit of the olive, a beautiful tree that can reach 15 meters high with a wide crown and a thick trunk, short and twisted.

This Mediterranean tree is considered native to Greece and Asia Minor, where there are still forests of wild olive trees. Its gray-silver fissured bark, and it's somewhat pointed lanceolate green leaves give it a unique beauty.

In the Mediterranean diet

Olive oil is one of the most important elements of the healthy Mediterranean diet. In fact, according to a publication in the journal Diabetes Spectrum, it is the main source of fat in this food model.

It has components that would offer health benefits, both as a culinary ingredient and for its therapeutic utility in its internal and external use. In addition, it has been considered a staple food, although only a few decades ago, science indicated its possible contribution to health.

In ancient times, civilizations such as the Egyptian, Greek or Roman, used it both for its culinary and medicinal qualities. In Greece, it acquired great commercial value, and they say that the Roman aristocracy highly valued the oil from the Iberian Peninsula.

Olive varieties

95% of olive cultivation is found in Mediterranean countries. In Spain, there are up to 260 varieties of this ancestral tree, being the main world producer of this appreciated oil.

Among the table olives, used for consumption as fruit, in snacks, salads, and other dishes, the best known in Spain are:

- Chamomile
- Gordon
- Hojiblanca
- Carrasqueña
- Cacereña

According to their color, we would highlight three types: green, purple, and black olives. All can act as treatments for heartburn. Oil is the juice extracted from olives, of which there are many varieties that give it a different flavor, smell, and properties.

Types of olive oil

There are different types of olive oil, depending on the mode of extraction or processing. The most appreciated oil with the greatest increase in demand is extra virgin olive oil (especially organic).

This variety is obtained by cold pressing, which is achieved naturally with a mechanical crushing and press process of the olive, extracting the oil with all its properties without needing to be refined.

The quality of the type of oil is defined not only by its taste or texture but by its degree of acidity and its greater or lesser percentage of antioxidants, vitamin E, polyphenols, beta-carotene, and other components that will give it greater biological value. This is influenced both by the ripening and quality of the olive, as well as the technology or machinery used.

Extra virgin olive oil

Considered of high quality, its acidity should not exceed 0.8 degrees. This acidity is in direct proportion to the free fatty acids and depends largely on the product manufacturing process. High acidity means defects in the olive, in the treatment, or in the conservation.

Virgin olive oil

At most, it reaches 2 degrees of acidity and is also

of great quality. The extraction procedure is the same as the previous one.

Lampante virgin

Its acidity exceeds 2 degrees, which does not make it suitable for consumption because of its bitter taste. Normally it goes through a refining process in which it loses acidity, but also its quality.

Refined Olive Oil

Because of its high acidity, either because the olive is not of good quality or due to the poor extraction process, it needs to go through a process to eliminate impurities that also remove its color, flavor, natural aroma, and many other properties. Of course, the acidity drops to 0.3 degrees.

Olive oil

A mixture of virgin and refined oil that reaches up to a degree of acidity and that contains some qualities of virgin oil but of much less quality.

Olive pomace oil

It is achieved through applying chemical products on the remains of olives that have already been pressed and ground, whereby an inedible crude pomace oil is obtained. It is mixed with refined lampante oil and results in less natural and less quality oil, which should not exceed a degree of acidity.

We recommend you bet on extra virgin olive oil; if it is organic, better. Even if it costs more in the long run, you win. We can consider it as an investment in health as well as pleasing the palate.

The king of the kitchen

Olive oil brings a very pleasant and characteristic aroma and flavor to dishes. Both raw and cooked food varies according to the type of olive oil used. We suggest trying several different brands raw, made with different types of olives so you can enjoy various culinary flavors.

Raw is used to:

- Dress salads, vegetables, and any other dish.
- At breakfast, to spread the toast with oil, salt, and tomato, as a side for sandwiches.
- Create sauces, cold soups, and starters.

Hot is used:

- For dressing stir-fry for stews and other stews, roasted in the oven of vegetables, fish, or meat.
- As an ingredient for making bread, cookies, biscuits, muffins, and all kinds of pastries.

In fried foods:

- It is convenient because it is not altered in high temperatures close to 200 degrees. In addition, cooked foods take their characteristic flavor and aroma, although they always lose properties in this process.

When it comes to frying, it is better not to smoke before putting the food and do not reuse the oil more than 5 times, if possible, with similar foods.

Nutritional value

We will distinguish two main sectors in its composition, fats (98%) and the rest. From the fats of olive oil, we can highlight that it has essential fatty acids for health. According to data collected in SELF Nutrition Data, it has monounsaturated, saturated, and polyunsaturated fatty acids:

- The mono-unsaturated are oleic acid (75%) and palmitoleic acid (1.5%).
- The saturated are palmitic acid and stearic acid (between 10 and 20%).
- The polyunsaturated are Linoleic acid (3 to 15%) and Linolenic acid (1.5%).

The rest of the components are hydrocarbons, beta-carotene (provitamin A), sterols, and tocopherols (vitamin E). Already in smaller quantities, it also has polyphenols that give it flavor, carotenes and chlorophyll that give it color, in addition to other volatile components that give it its peculiar smell.

Properties for health

A single tablespoon of extra virgin olive oil a day

gives us 60 calories without cholesterol. In addition, as supported by a publication in the medical journal Maturitas, it would help prevent cardiovascular disease by providing antioxidants and a portion of the recommended dose of vitamin E.

Among the antioxidants are the polyphenols that protect the heart, reducing the action of free radicals and preventing plaques from attaching in the arteries, in addition to having an anti-inflammatory effect. Each tablespoon has 7 grams of fat, of which most are unsaturated, which makes olive oil a great contribution of "good fats."

The recommended dose would be about 40 grams a day, which is equivalent to two or three tablespoons. Among its benefits, we can highlight:

Cardiovascular

Olive oil in its composition is rich in oleic acid (between 60-80%), which is a mono-unsaturated fat considered beneficial for the body, especially for the circulatory system. A study published in Endocrine, Metabolic & Immune Disorders concluded that it could contribute to reducing the atherosclerotic burden.

Bone health

Regular consumption of olive oil would be beneficial in promoting bone health. According to the conclusions of a study published in the journal,

Nutrients, dietary intake of olive oil would be positively associated with the prevention of problems such as osteoporosis. Specifically, it would help maintain bone density, especially in adult women.

Anti-inflammatory

Chronic inflammation is one of the factors associated with the development of multiple diseases. For this reason, the inclusion of natural products such as extra virgin olive oil in the usual diet is recommended.

In fact, a study in the scientific journal, Nature, highlighted that extra virgin olive oil would contain an antioxidant known as oleocanthal, which has demonstrated effects similar to ibuprofen, a popular anti-inflammatory medication.

Other benefits of olive oil

As compiled by research published through the International Journal of Molecular Sciences, olive oil would have other important health benefits, many of which are attributed to its content of polyphenols and healthy fats. The most important would be:

- Helps modulate the immune system.
- Improves metabolic health.
- Encourages control of high blood pressure and high cholesterol levels.

- Helps fight free radicals.

Promote the health of patients with diabetes.

Did you know this information about olive oil? As you can see, it is a source of fat that you should include in your diet. However, we advise you to consult a nutritionist to determine what amount to take and how.

CHAPTER 8

BREAKFAST LOAF & BUN

1.   Pudding Oat Protein Bagels (Mini form)

Ingredients:

- 125g cream cheese, lean
- 1 dash of apple cider vinegar
- 125 ml of milk
- 1 egg
- 20 grams of whole milk powder (or skimmed milk powder)
- 1 heaped teaspoon of bourbon vanilla custard powder
- 25 grams Whey Isolate "Cookies & Cream" or "Vanilla."
- 25 grams of oat bran
- 15 grams of bamboo fiber or fiberfill
- 8 grams of psyllium husk
- 15 grams of ground almonds
- 1 teaspoon of baking powder
- One pinch of natron

Preparation:

1. Preheat oven to 160 degrees, put out mini bagel mold or muffin mold and grease if necessary.
2. Stir the pudding powder in a two teaspoon microwavable bowl until smooth. Cook the remaining milk and oat bran in the

microwave to a pulp.

3. In the meantime, add the cream cheese with the apple cider vinegar to the mixing bowl.
4. Mix the finished porridge with the cream cheese and check the temperature: it should not be too hot before adding to the egg. Possibly. Just let cool for five minutes and then stir in the egg.
5. Mix the remaining dry ingredients well in a separate bowl.
6. With the blender running, add the dry ingredients to the cream cheese mixture until a smooth dough is formed.
7. Pour the dough into the molds and let it swell for 5 to 10 minutes, then put it in the oven with it.
8. On medium track, at 160 degrees, bake the bagels for 18 minutes. At the first baking try, I recommend a Garprobe. The pudding oat bagels should stay light so you can toast them without burning them.

2. Low carb Ciabatta with extra protein

Ingredients:

- 1 pack of Almond bread mix ciabatta
- 40 grams Whey isolate, neutral
- 50 grams of butter, melted and slightly cooled
- 420 ml of water
- 2 egg yolks
- 1 heaped tablespoon of finely chopped herbs of your choice
- ½ pack sourdough extract (optional, is only flavor carrier.) Not typical ciabatta, but I love the gentle rye taste
- ½ teaspoon salt
- Bamboo fiber for dusting dough pieces

Preparation:

1. Preheat the oven according to the package preparations, line the baking tray with paper or permanent baking foil, and prepare.
2. Mix moist ingredients in the food processor or with the blender.
3. Mix dry ingredients well in a separate bowl and mix quickly with the wet ingredients. The result is a shapeable dough.
4. Share with wet hands in 6-10 rolls, depending on the desired size. I rolled 8 medium-sized rolls.

5. Dust with bamboo fiber and use the roll stamp (or cut with the knife as desired).
6. Off in the oven for 55 minutes.
7. Allow to cool, done.

3. Red Pesto Protein Bagels

Ingredients:

- 200 ml of egg white
- 1 tablespoon of apple cider vinegar
- 120 g of skimmed quark or protein quark
- 120 g of red pesto in the glass
- 3 drops Tabasco, hot (optional)
- 1 heaped tablespoon of Parmesan
- 1 heaped tablespoon of fresh, Italian herbs
- 60 grams Whey Isolate, neutral
- 50 grams of almond flour, de-oiled
- 10 grams of psyllium husk
- 1 heaped teaspoon of baking powder
- ½ teaspoon of soda

Optional: sesame to sprinkle.

Preparation:

1. Preheat oven to 160 degrees, put out big bagel shape.
2. Mix moist ingredients, including the herbs in the food processor or with a blender.
3. Mix dry ingredients well in a separate bowl and then add them to the wet ingredients one tablespoon at a time while mixing.
4. Let the dough swell for 5 - 10 minutes.
5. Divide the dough into the bagel shape and bake the bagels at 160 °C for about 25 minutes.

6. Remove the bagels from the mold as soon as possible after baking. In the case of the good bagel form, this is immediate, with the cheap forms, please wait 5 minutes, so that you can take out the babies undamaged. Let it cool on a grate.

7. As always: Before consumption, freshly toast or grill - best to cut the bagel and toast the halves individually, then they are crunchy outside and soft inside.

4. Protein Sandwich Toast from the Tin

Ingredients:

- 200 grams of egg white
- 30 grams of melted butter (Optional! Can be omitted to save calories)
- 180 grams of quark
- 35 grams of potato fibers
- 1 tablespoon of psyllium husk
- 50 grams of Whey Isolate
- 1 tablespoon of apple cider vinegar
- 10 grams of calcium citrate
- 2 sachets of dry yeast (Only as flavor! Does not have to go)
- 1 teaspoon of baking powder
- 1 pinch of natron
- 1 level teaspoon of potassium salt or normal salt

Optional: bagel spice or sesame to sprinkle

Preparation:

1. Preheat the oven to 160 °C, line the baking tray with baking paper
2. Mix all moist ingredients together. Make sure the melted butter cools down a bit, so the fat doesn't clot.
3. In a separate bowl, mix well all the dry ingredients except the topping for sprinkling.

4. Mix the dry ingredients under the wet ingredients, in tablespoons, until a smooth dough is formed.
5. Let the dough swell for about 5 to 10 minutes to allow the fibers to do their job.
6. Quickly pour the dough on the baking tray, smooth it nicely. Make sure the dough is about half a centimeter high. This portion does not fill the entire baking tray!
7. The dough comes on the middle rail in the oven; mine was after 18 minutes through. The chopsticks test on the first baking attempt saves from raw dough.
8. Before toasting, please use a toaster for your toast, so that it is crispy on the outside and soft on the inside. That's why I recommend not baking the sandwiches in the oven too dark, so they do not burn in the toaster.
9. Once the low carb butter toast is cooked through, get the tin out of the oven and cut squares in the desired size with a pizza roller. I recommend cutting the dough sheet into 9-12 squares, depending on your personal stomach size.
10. With a dough lifter, put the hot toast on a rack to cool down.
11. Finished.

5. Protein Oatmeal Bagels

Ingredients (for 6 mini bagels, 60 grams):

- 125g thin quark
- 125 ml of milk
- 1 egg
- 25 grams of sweet whey protein (Vanilla Whey or Cookies & Cream Whey)
- 15 grams of ground almonds
- 12 grams of bamboo fiber (or 20 grams of potato)
- 10 grams of psyllium husks
- 25 grams of oat bran
- 1 teaspoon of baking powder
- 1 pinch of soda
- ½ tablespoon of apple cider vinegar

Alternatives:

Whey Isolate goes any kind or tasteless, to bake little sweet bagels that also go with cheese. Due to oats and milk, the milk protein bagels are rather sweet even without sweet protein powder and are not suitable for very savory toppings. Those who only have neutral whey can also use low carb sweetener or flavor to get the flavor they want.

Preparing the oatmeal bagels

Preparation:

1. Boil the oat bran with 75 ml of milk to a pulp. This is best done in the microwave. Let the porridge cool down a bit.

2. Preheat the oven to 150 °C, prepare the form for small bagels/donuts.

3. While the oat bran chill is cooling, mix all the remaining ingredients to a uniform mass and add the lukewarm (or chilled) oatmeal to finish.

4. Fill the mixture into the 6 small molds. If you do not have a bagel shape, go for the Burger Bun shape in an S or muffin shape.

5. Let the dough swell in the molds for 5 minutes and then place in the oven for about 25 minutes. The milk bagels taste delicious in bright! They are then juicy like a quark ball inside, and fluffy by the psyllium and fibers.

6. Cheese Ham Protein Bagels

Ingredients:

- 220 grams of egg white
- 1 tablespoon of apple cider vinegar
- 180 grams of protein quark or lean quark
- 100 grams of grated cheese (16% fat)
- 75 grams of cured ham, diced
- 50 grams Whey Isolate, neutral
- 40 grams of bamboo fiber or potato fiber
- 30 grams of parmesan, grated
- 1 packet of dry yeast (aroma, can be omitted)
- 2 garlic cloves, pressed
- 5 grams of psyllium husk
- ½ packet of baking powder
- 1 pinch of natron

Preparation:

1. Preheat oven to 160 degrees, make bagel shape, stand out.
2. Mix dry ingredients and wet ingredients in separate bowls. Then mix the dry ingredients with the wet ingredients one tablespoon at a time. The dough should be allowed to soak for 10 minutes so that the psyllium husk and bamboo fiber have time to absorb the liquid well. To make these bagels nice and fluffy, you should definitely give this time. I fill the mass to swell directly

into the bagel mold, so I can place the sheet directly in the oven.

3. The baking time at 160 degrees circulating air is about 25 minutes. As the "first baker" of the protein bagels, you should do a Garprobe with chopsticks! Every oven bakes differently, and you want the bagels baked through but still very juicy.

4. When the bagels are ready, let them cool on a grill. Make sure to halve immediately before eating, so that the bagel is crispy on the outside and juicy, soft on the inside, as a bagel should be.

5. Tips: Can it be a few more calories? Full-fat grated cheese and bacon instead of pork ham pimp the bagels and make them even more delicious. Personally, I do not like it that much, but that does not apply to you. Every now and then these may be feasted.

7. Tiger nuts High Protein Bagels

Ingredients:

- 200 grams of egg white
- 180 grams of protein quark or lean quark
- 1 tablespoon of apple cider vinegar
- 50 grams Whey isolate
- 60 grams of ground almonds, roasted
- 10 grams of bamboo fiber
- 10 grams of psyllium husk
- 1 teaspoon of baking powder
- 1 teaspoon of soda
- 1 packet of dry yeast (aroma, can be omitted)

Optional:

Chopped tiger nuts or hazelnuts to sprinkle the bagels

Preparation:

1. Preheat oven to 160 degrees, provide bagel shape
2. Mix dry and moist ingredients well apart from each other. Then add the dry ingredients to the moist ingredients whilst the blender is working, one tablespoon at a time. The dough should "swell" for about 10 minutes after mixing so that the bagels get the right consistency.

3. Spread the swollen dough onto the four bagel pans and bake in the oven for about 25 minutes until golden yellow bagels emerge. Please do the chopstick tasting the first time you try a protein bagel recipe. The dough should still be juicy but no longer sticky.

4. The most important step to the fantastic protein bagel: Halve the bagel before serving and toast it! It should be crunchy on the outside and soft and fluffy on the inside.

8. Hemp Zucchini Bagel

Ingredients:

- 200 grams of egg white
- 150 grams of protein quark or lean quark
- 1 tablespoon of apple cider vinegar
- 50 grams Whey isolate neutral
- 20 grams of collagen hydrolyzate neutral
- 50 grams of hemp flour
- 50 grams of grated carrot
- 100 grams of grated zucchini, well expressed
- 10 grams of psyllium husk
- 1 packet of dry yeast (as a flavor, you can simply omit)
- 1 pinch of natron

Preparation:

1. Preheat the oven to 160 degrees.
2. Rub the zucchini and carrot and place it on a strainer. Salt and let stand for 10 minutes. Then firmly squeeze the liquid from the vegetables with a clean dishcloth or a cheesecloth.
3. Mix all moist ingredients, including the vegetable grated in a large bowl; mix all dry ingredients in a small bowl.
4. While the blender is running, add the dry ingredients to the wet ingredients one teaspoonful until a smooth dough is formed.

The consistency is similar to the batter. Let the dough swell for 5 to 10 minutes.

5. Distribute the dough into the bagel form, because there the dough reliably comes out without fats.
6. After about 25 minutes, the bagels are through. Do the chopstick test if it's your first protein bagels.
7. After baking, quickly remove the bagels from the silicone mold and let them cool on a grill.
8. Protein bagels should be halved and toasted before consumption. So on the outside, they're crunchy and inside they're fluffy like a bagel should.

9. Parsnip Mini Bagels

Ingredients:

- 200g egg white
- 180g skim quark or protein quark (Skyr goes too)
- 70g Whey Isolate (neutral)
- 50g bamboo fiber or potato fiber
- 10g psyllium husk
- 1 packet of baker's yeast, dry (only as flavor, you can omit)
- 1 tablespoon of apple cider vinegar
- 1 pinch of natron
- 1 go teaspoon of tartar baking soda or normal baking soda
- 100 grams of grated parsnip

Preparation:

1. Preheat the oven to 160 degrees, if necessary, grease the silicone mold (if you take the donut, as I do - just grease the thing, which is very cheap and works well, but it has to be greased every time).
2. Mix the wet and dry ingredients separately. Then add the dry ingredients one tablespoon at a time with the mixer/food processor to the wet ingredients.
3. Let that dough swell for a couple of minutes. If you're hectic, you can skip the step. I think they get swollen for a nicer consistency.

4. For me, the bagels need 20 minutes at 160 degrees air circulation. Do a chopstick test if it's your first protein bagels.
5. The most important tip: The bagels are halved in the toaster before eating. Then on the ground, they're crunchy and stay fluffy inside, just like a true bagel!

10. Protein Bagel With Cream Cheese And Berries

Ingredients:

- Half (or whole) protein bagel
- 30 grams of cream cheese with the fat level of your choice
- A handful of berries
- 5 g (about one teaspoon) of hazelnut sauce for the extra portion of good fat and flavor
- Tonka bean, vanilla or similar on request.

Preparation:

1. Toast the bagel for this Serving a little darker. I like it nice and golden brown. The crust then becomes crispy, leaving the interior soft and pleasant.
2. Coat half with 30 grams of cream cheese and cover with the berries. If you want to treat yourself to something special, rub a little tonka bean over it. Alternatively, you can mix the vanilla pulp with cream cheese. Vanilla & Co. are optional.
3. As a topping, drizzle the hazelnut or other good fat of your choice on the bag and you are done with the dream breakfast.

11. Low carb Protein Milk Rolls aka High Protein Bagels with Chocolate Drops

Ingredients:

- 220 grams of egg white
- 180 grams of lean quark or protein quark vanilla
- 1 tablespoon of apple cider vinegar
- 30 grams of chocolate drops with xylitol (or other low carb chocolate)
- 35 grams of potato fibers
- 50 grams of Vanilla Whey Isolate
- 15 grams of psyllium husk
- 10 grams of ground almonds (optional, adding good fat)
- Mark a ½ vanilla pod
- 1 teaspoon of baking powder
- 1 pinch of natron
- 8 drops of butter biscuit flavor (optional)

Preparation:

1. Preheat oven to 170 degrees and prepare baking pan. I use the Lurch baking mold for bagels. You can bake the chocolate crumbs without carbohydrates but also as small muffins or in any other form of your choice.
2. Set aside chocolate drops. Mix the remaining dry ingredients in a bowl and weigh the wet ingredients with the vanilla pulp in another bowl.

3. Beat the wet ingredients with the food processor or the hand mixer to a smooth mass, adding the dry ingredients at least one tablespoon at a time.
4. Let the dough swell for 10 minutes so that the psyllium husk makes it thicker. The consistency is like batter.
5. Only half fill the bagel form with the dough, spread the chocolate drops over it, and cover with the remaining dough. The chocolate drops should not be visible.
6. Leave in the oven for 25 minutes. Do not forget the stick sample! The low carb chocolate crumbs are ready when the bagel is golden brown on the outside and there is no more dough on the stick.
7. Remove the bagels from the oven and remove them carefully from the hot mold. In the silicone molds, the bagels sweat very fast, and that makes the dough too wet.
8. The chocolate rolls are best cut and toasted. With the Xylit Schokodrops, I had no problems that they melt in the toaster. I do not know what that looks like with other products. If in doubt, just use the bread roll of your toaster and toast the bagel as a whole.

12. High Protein Oat Bagels

Ingredients:

- 220 grams of egg white
- 180 grams of protein quark (or lean quark)
- 1 tablespoon of apple cider vinegar
- 1 tablespoon of flaxseed, crushed
- 50 grams of tender oatmeal, ground or finished oatmeal
- 50 grams of protein powder
- 15 grams of psyllium husk
- 1 teaspoon Baking powder
- 1 pinch of natron
- 1 Tl. Salt (best potassium salt)
- 10 grams of FiberFin Resistant Strength

Optional: 1 pack of Dry yeast. This gives the Bagel a typical yeast aroma.

Preparation:

1. Preheat the oven to 160 degrees, prepare the bagel mold. Alternatively, you can divide this recipe into 8 small form troughs. For the little bagels, I have bagel shapes, and they are ok and cheap - please grease very easily). Especially for less than six months operated "stomachs," it's a good plan.
2. Mix all dry ingredients well in a bowl. The baking soda and soda should be evenly distributed.

3. Mix the moist ingredients in a second large mixing bowl and mix everything with a hand mixer or food processor to a uniform mass.
4. Add the dry ingredients one spoon at a time with the blender running until a smooth dough is formed.
5. Approve the dough and give it 10 minutes rest to swell the fiber (it does not open), then put it in the bag mold and in the preheated oven. The consistency of the dough is more fluid than batter.
6. In my oven at 160 °C, the bagels took 38 minutes to brown outside, and the stick sample returned without sticky dough.
7. Remove the bagels carefully after baking immediately from the silicone mold. The dough is softer and juicier than normal baked goods anyway and should not sweat in the form if possible. From a high-quality shape, you can easily remove the bagels with a little sensibility immediately!
8. The High Protein Bagels taste best toasted - that's the way it is with most low carb rolls and bread. For freezing, I recommend you to cut the bagels with a sharp knife already and freeze flat side by side. If they are frozen through, the halves can lie over each other again, for example, in a bag or a freezer. You can remove them individually and crunch them in the toaster within 3-4 minutes.

13. Low Carb Toast with Potato Fiber

Ingredients:

Wet ingredients

- 200 grams of egg white (or whole eggs, but then egg white tastes good)
- 160 grams of lean quark
- 1 tablespoon of apple cider vinegar

Dry ingredients

- 35 grams of potato fiber
- 30 grams Whey Protein neutral
- 10 grams of psyllium husk
- 1 level teaspoon of soda
- 3 grams of tartar baking soda or baking soda (tartar tastes better)
- granulated teaspoon salt (e.g., potassium salt)

Optional ingredients (can be omitted)

- 10 grams of calcium citrate optional,

strengthens the dough and provides calcium

- a packet of dry yeast optional as a flavor

Preparation:

1. Preheat the oven to 180 degrees. Remove the silicone mold for muffins or grease the normal muffin tin! The dough is very low in fat and does not go out of shape—paper cups do not work because everything sticks to them. The best is a silicone mold. Disconnect the hand mixer or food processor. I always use a food processor.
2. Mix dry ingredients well in a bowl. The baking soda and soda should be well distributed.
3. Place moist ingredients in the bowl of the food processor or in a large mixing bowl. Gradually stir in the dry ingredients before producing a uniform flour. The consistency of the dough is like batter.
4. Let the dough rest for 5-10 minutes; the psyllium absorbs some liquid in time.
5. Pour batter into the muffin molds. I always distribute it on 9-10 molds. Then put in the preheated oven for 25 minutes. A swab sample is recommended!
6. Remove from the oven and quickly free from the silicone mold. This is already after 2-3 minutes; the protein toasties fall out quite voluntarily. Allow to cool slightly, push into the toaster, and then enjoy it.

14. Protein Fitness Bread

Protein bread from healthy ingredients simply baked yourself is sure of taste. Of course, the taste is not comparable to wheat bread; the consistency is a bit juicier; through the resistant starch and the psyllium, it is a bit looser than bread only from quark and oat bran.

Preparation:

1. Preheat the oven to 180 degrees. Line box shape with baking paper.
2. Turn out food processor with a whisk.

Preparation:

1. Put all wet ingredients in the mixing bowl and whisk. Mix dry ingredients in a separate bowl.
2. Put tablespoonfuls of the dry ingredients while the food processor is running in the quark mixture. Let the dough rest for 2 minutes.
3. Pour the dough into the box and immediately put it in the preheated oven.

Baking time

Bake in the lower third of the oven for 50 minutes. Make a stick sample. My bread took 55 minutes in the oven.

The bread should cool well before cutting, otherwise it crumbles or breaks apart. To do this, allow the protein bread to cool in the mold for about 10 minutes, then gently drop it onto a griddle and remove the baking paper. Note: When baking in a silicone mold, the pastry tends to become slightly "damp" if it cools in the mold too long after baking. Therefore, after using the silicone for a few minutes, I would then—carefully—push the bread out of the mold.

Well toasted, the bread tastes best! As a result, it gets a "snappy" crust with delicious roasted aromas and remains moist inside, just like fresh bread. Glorious. I'm not a fan of classic cold cuts and recommend topping with vegetables or a dollop of jam.

CHAPTER 9

PROTEIN SOUP

Kohlrabi Jerusalem Artichoke Cream Soup

Using the example of my vegetable soup with kohlrabi, Jerusalem artichoke, and a small portion of potato, I'll show you how to make a creamy soup with an egg that looks and tastes creamy and brings extra protein for gastric bypass or tube stomach.

Ingredients:

For the soup

- 150 grams of kohlrabi
- 100 grams of Jerusalem artichoke
- 50 grams of potato
- 300 milliliters of chicken broth or vegetable stock

For the bond

- 2 eggs (size M or L)
- 20 grams of collagen hydrolyzate or instant protein (e.g., Adozan or allin pure protein)

Toppings

- 1 teaspoon of pumpkin seed oil per person (or borage oil, argan oil, olive oil, linseed oil)
- 1 teaspoon of pumpkin seeds per person
- Protein cream soup

Preparations:

1. Clean vegetables and dice them. Cook with broth in the microwave or in a pot.
2. In the meantime, prepare blender and add 2 eggs and the protein directly.
3. Place the lid on the blender and mix the egg with protein powder. This step is optional; I always do it that way.
4. We will now put the ready-cooked vegetable brewing mix in the running blender. For this, you open only the small in the lid, usually a transparent plug or the like.
5. Put the blender in medium, add a good tablespoon of broth, and another until a creamy consistency has formed. Once you have mixed about 1/3 of the liquid with the egg-protein mix, you can add the rest with vegetables with a ladle in larger spoons.
6. If the soup is fine enough for you, you can turn off the blender and pour it into individual bowls. The portion is enough for about 4 meals if you have a gastric bypass or stomach. For "normal" stomachs, it is more like two portions.
7. Finally, add a teaspoon of high-quality vegetable oil to the soup, scatter a few pumpkin seeds or something similar on it and enjoy your quick and easy protein cream soup.

Attention: warm-up and freeze

If you do not plaster the four portions of soup together with your family right away, you may want to freeze them or warm them up later.

Storage in the refrigerator would work without problems for two days if you had given the soup boiling into the egg mass. Make sure the soup is quickly cooled down and airtight in the bottom compartment of the refrigerator.

When warming up, the soup must not cook. In the pot, warm gently while stirring; in the microwave, put on low wattage first for a minute, then stir and gently heat gradually until it is hot but not boiling.

What happens when the protein soup boils up?

The egg whites flake out again. It does not change the taste but it is not visually pleasing. The simple solution is to purée the soup in a small blender again. Since this annoys me, I avoid the situation in which I supervise the soup when warming up.

Basic Recipe "Soup Kit"

Vegetable serving

2x a serving of vegetables, 50 grams. Of course, you can only work with one vegetable variety and then take 100 grams. The single preparation provides a lot of variety on your plate. When making your selection, you may want to eat some light foods shortly after surgery to avoid bloating and digestive problems.

Source of protein

50 grams of protein source: for example, lean cream cheese/feta/mozzarella grated/lean minced meat/fish/canned tuna/cooked ham/chicken breast cold cuts/legumes (if tolerated) etc.

Protein source and binding agent for creaminess

- 1 egg size M

Liquid

- 100 ml broth to taste

Serving size

This results in 2 servings, 150 grams undiluted. I diluted soups a little more in the first two weeks to make them easier to slip through the minimizer ring of my gastric bypass.

Everyone fine-tunes themselves. Also, the amount of food differs from person to person—so stay relaxed, if you can easily eat more or less than the 150 grams.

Warm-up and durability

Personally, I recommend eating fresh soup on the same day. When warming up, select a low level of the microwave and stir first every 30 seconds. If the soup is already reasonably hot, stop every 10 seconds. The soup can "flocculate" with a strong boil.

This does not affect the quality of the egg whites—it's just not that nice visually. Just give an extra round into the blender, and it's done. Since the extra dishes get dirty (I hate that), I'm careful when heating.

Preparations:

1. Dice vegetables (if necessary) and place in a

large microwave-proof bowl

2. Add the stock and microwave until the vegetables are cooked.
3. If you have raw meat or raw fish for the soup, chop it into small pieces or mince in chunks and add the mixture of vegetables and broth. The cooking time is extended by 1-2 minutes.
4. While the vegetables are cooking, add your protein source and an egg to the blender and purée both very finely. The egg helps to make especially cooked meat, ham, or cooked fish a very fine paste.
5. Do you cook your meat/fish in the microwave? Then just put the egg in the blender and continue with this guide.
6. Place the broth from the boiled vegetables in a separate container and serve.
7. Turn the blender back to medium and pour the boiling broth into your egg-protein mixture. The heat cooks the egg and forms an outstanding soup base without carbohydrates.
8. When the broth is completely inside, stop the mixer for a moment, add the boiled vegetables (and possibly the fish/meat cooked in the soup) and purée the soup as finely as you want it to be.
9. The soup is now ready and can be eaten directly. If you want them hot, warm the soup up gently. Decorated with a dollop of low-fat yogurt, the soup tastes twice as good.

10. Do not forget to add a teaspoon (about 5 milliliters) of healthy fat to your soup before serving. Do you not know which fat is suitable? "Essential fatty acids that you should also eat every day when you lose weight" shows you the best options for healthy fat after gastric reduction.

The raw egg and the soup

Since there may be some concern that you have a raw egg in the soup: the heat of the broth and vegetables cooks the egg through. If you are very anxious, you can boil the soup gently after puréeing.

CHAPTER 10

PROTEIN COFFEE

Protein "Matcha Latte"

Matcha is one of the not so new "superfoods" and has conquered as a latte a permanent place on the map of the big coffee house. Recently, the powdered green tea lurks in ice cream, pastries, and all sorts of sweets. The trend is coming—where else—from Japan and Germans seem to depend on it.

Ingredients:

- 300 ml of milk
- 1 teaspoon matcha powder
- 30 ml of hot water
- 5 grams of protein powder vanilla (or to taste)
- 10 grams of collagen or a collagen mix
- High protein matcha latte superfood

Preparations:

1. The preparation is as easy as Protein Latte Macchiato. Make milk hot, froth with protein.
2. Mix Matcha Powder with 30 ml of hot water until smooth and pour carefully over a spoon into the hot milk.

Protein Coffee Light - Low-Calorie Alternative

Protein coffee in the "Latte Macchiato" variant counts, due to the calories, as a snack. The Protein Coffee's Light Recipe is for those who like to drink coffee often and are not satisfied with 1-2 servings instead of another protein snack.

Ingredients:

Main ingredients

- 90 ml of espresso
- 50 ml of boiling water
- 150 ml minus L protein milk (low-fat, high-protein, and foams well)
- 10 grams Whey hydrolyzate or other whey protein neutral or with flavor

Optional ingredients

- 2-3 drops of aromatic drops
- 1 pinch of cinnamon or cocoa (for dusting)
- Protein coffee calorie-reduced

Preparations:

1. Prepare espresso/filter coffee. If you use filter coffee, a low-acid, mild variety is best.
2. Heat milk as usual. The milk must be very hot, but not allowed to cook.
3. Bring water to a boil.
4. The hot milk in the electric Shake mixer or with the blender (or such a little electrical

thing for milk frothing) with the protein powder very quickly stirs up.

5. Add hot water to the beaker, stir gently.
6. Infuse espresso. If you need something sweet—but please try it the first time! The lactose-free milk provides a lot of protein and low fat, tastes a little sweeter than "normal" milk.

Protein Cocoa Recipe Without Milk

Protein cocoa - hot chocolate with lots of protein.

I love coffee. If only there was not the little "but." Sometimes I do not want caffeine in the afternoon—maybe I feel like some chocolate.

Chocolate delivers calories primarily from fat and sugar—in moderation, it may also time on the table. Nevertheless, I often avoid them and opt for protein cocoa.

Protein Hot Chocolate is not low in calories!

The reality in advance: A protein cocoa without milk does not have much fewer calories than a small bar of chocolate (15-20 grams), which comes around with 80-100 calories, depending on the type.

So it's a protein-rich snack!

In my recipe for hot chocolate without milk, I give two alternatives: Preparation with water and preparation with water and egg. The "egg cocoa" is derived from a classic recipe of the ketogenic diet, namely the egg-milk.

Eggs and boiling water are emulsified together in a blender. Together with vanilla, a pinch of salt, and a pinch of cinnamon, this results in low-carbohydrate milk of high-quality protein, which is even suitable for coffee.

If you are a patient after a gastric reduction, you can simply do without the addition of coconut oil, butter, etc.

Tip: Of course, the recipe also works with cow's milk or other plant milk.

Ingredients:

- 150 ml of water
- 1 egg (optional omit!)
- 15 grams of protein powder
- 5 grams of cocoa powder, heavily de-oiled
- 1 pinch of salt
- 1 pinch of cinnamon
- Protein coffee as an intermediate meal

Preparation:

Preparation with egg

1. Put the egg with the protein powder, the cinnamon, the cocoa powder and the salt in the blender—or in a tall container, if you want to use a blender.
2. Bring water to a boil.
3. Turn on the blender and whisk up the egg with the other ingredients. Then pour the boiling water into the mixing vessel in a fine stream while the blender is running. It is very important that the mixer runs at least at medium speed while pouring water. Only

then will you manage an emulsion without lumps, and the egg does not stop.

4. Finished

Preparation without egg

Here you just leave the egg, and you can also work with an electric Shake mixer or similar to mix the powder with water, vegetable milk, or milk.

Protein Chai Latte

Drinks with hot milk are the hype par excellence. Not only coffee houses offer them, but also at home, treat yourself more and more gourmet coffee and tea specialties. For a real chai, I'm too lazy; it will not be authentic here.

But this chai brings an extra dose of protein.

I would like to infuse the chai like a latte macchiato. Of course, you can also cook the tea bags in the milk. I like it so much better.

Ingredients:

- 3 tea bags Chai tea of your choice (I prefer Cacao Chai)
- 50 ml of water
- 200 ml of milk
- 15 grams of protein powder
- chai latte protein

Preparation:

1. Boil the water and pour over the tea bags. We make a kind of "tea" espresso. Let the tea soak for 8-10 minutes.
2. Just before the end of the brewing time, heat up the milk. It should be very hot but not boiling.
3. Incidentally, the protein in the protein powder is not "destroyed" by heat for our body; it only changes its consistency. The

actual amino acids (the form in which the body absorbs the protein) remain intact!

4. Not letting the milk boil properly only prevents clumping, just changing the consistency. Lumps in the tea are just not nice.

5. Add the protein powder to the hot milk and froth up the mixture in a shake mixer vigorously. Alternatively, of course, use an electric milk frother (a small thing that once had the triumph of the cappuccino for everyone in the household ... who remembers?). If you want to sweeten, this is a perfect time. By mixing the sweetness, it is distributed evenly.

6. Check the temperature of your tea concentrate. If the tea has cooled too much, heat it gently. (Do not put a tea bag with a metal clip in the microwave).

7. Pour the strong tea over a spoon into the frothed milk. Finished.

Protein coffee recipe Latte Macchiato

Protein coffee is a coffee variant with a lot of protein. It is ideal for drinking the daily portion of protein powder after a gastric bypass or stomach. As a portion, I use 2 portions. The first days and weeks after surgery, drinking is a challenge for some operators. A protein drink with 200 milliliters (half portion of the recipe) is sufficient. Later, you determine the right composition, in which you estimate how much protein you lack without the coffee.

Ingredients:

- 300 milliliters of milk of your choice
- 8 grams of whey protein powder (with or without taste)
- 10 grams of collagen hydrolyzate or instant protein (or Adozan 100, allin pure protein)
- 60 - 90 milliliters of espresso (or filter coffee as desired)

Optional

- 4 grams of inulin (soluble fiber)
- 1 gram of cocoa powder (for dusting)
- Protein coffee which shakes

Preparation:

1. Put on coffee.
2. Heat the milk. The liquid should be very hot, but not boil!

3. Place the milk in a high mixing bowl or the beaker of an electric shaker mixer. Add protein powder to it and immediately on a high level. If you do not have an electric shake mixer, you can use a blender or a milk frother.

CHAPTER 11

HIGH PROTEIN PUDDING

Protein mousse

Protein Mousse - The trick for beauty

Protein Mousse is made easy and tastes delicious like a creamy, creamy dessert. In our case, without cream and unnecessary calories.

Where does the recipe of the protein mousse originally come from?

Protein Mousse - originally from the ketogenic diet

You will be astonished if I mention the ancient Atkins program as a source. Yes, Atkins—you read that right. Of course, the recipe is not called protein mousse but had some "protein-free" and "fat" name, and the preparation deviated slightly from my protein mousse recipe.

Protein Mousse - typical for fat fasting

But here comes the inspiration. In my keto phase around 2012, I prepared this recipe in the ketogenic variant very happily as a dessert.

With jelly, fat sources such as cream or MCT oil were puréed, the mixture was once again cold for half an hour, and a fluffy and high-calorie mousse with moderate protein content was ready on the table.

Especially when fat fasting, many people used the mousse to mix high-fat food with low carbohydrates and protein.

Keto is great for people with stomach reduction but not necessarily ideal

Ketogenic nutrition is only suitable to a limited extent after gastric reduction. We, therefore, prepare our protein mousse with skim quark or skyr. Trust me, it tastes delicious and delivers a protein-rich snack.

Protein Mousse instead of Cream Mousse after Gastric Bypass & Co.

The pleasant consistency provides a change from the daily quark yogurt battle. Due to the high water content, this meal slips very quickly through the new stomach pouch. That is so wanted! It may well be that you can do more in volume than you expect in advance because of the consistency. Stay relaxed, that's normal and completely alright. It does not mean that your stomach has widened.

Protein Beauty Mousse - great for skin, hair and nails with a trick

In the protein mousse is collagen hydrolyzate or, e.g., Adozan as a protein is especially good, because it dissolves very well and does not cause a significant off-taste.

Combine Vitamin C with your protein mousse. Either as a powder (you get in the drugstore) or directly as a fruit topping such as kiwi.

Collagen and Vitamin C help support collagen formation in your body and can help keep your hair, skin, and connective tissues fit.

Beauty comes from within—and proverbially. From the outside, you can "smear on it" as much as you want—as your body is built, that's what really matters.

Ingredients:

Results in about one serving // very shortly after surgery, if necessary sufficient for 2 servings

- 120 grams of cooked and firm jello, sugar-free
- 2 tablespoons lemon juice
- 100 grams of skinny quark, Skyr or lean Greek yogurt
- 1 tablespoon of collagen or other "clear" protein powder
- Sweetener according to need and taste

Optional: 120 mg Vitamin C powder

Preparation:

1. The preparation is very simple.
2. Purée all ingredients together until a uniform mass is obtained. The mass is slightly liquid.
3. Put the mass in a bowl and put the protein mousse in the fridge for at least half an hour. You can also prepare, e.g., several portions and store in preserving jars/bowls with lid portioned in the refrigerator for 2 - 3 days.

High protein pudding

Ehrmann's High Protein Pudding is delicious, and one of the products that are on everyone's lips on Instagram. The binders contain the protein-rich pudding from the refrigerated shelf but also additives, which I like to avoid.

My High Protein Pudding recipe is indicated with 4 servings of protein pudding. This quantity refers to a portion size of 95 ml volume and is aimed at people who have had their new stomach for only a few weeks. Since I personally like the pudding with fruit (the first 2 weeks after surgery boiled and seedless) or topping yogurt, I have chosen four small portions of just under 100 grams.

It's fine if you can eat a 200 - 250 ml portion months after surgery!

High Protein Pudding is easy to make yourself. You can use cow's milk or plant milk for the production, and you have the protein choice as the free choice.

Ingredients:

- 300 ml of milk
- 40 grams of slightly soluble protein powder
- 17.5 grams of custard powder, variety to taste (without added sugar)
- 10 grams of inulin (can be omitted)
- The sweetness of your choice and taste
- Protein nut nougat pudding recipe

Preparation:

1. Put the small pot on the stove.

2. Stir the pudding powder with 50 ml of milk, the sweet and the inulin.

3. Separate the protein powder with 50 ml of milk from the custard smooth (stir depending on the powder from very creamy to viscous).

4. Whisk until ready.

Cook the pudding

1. Bring remaining milk (200 ml) to the boil in the pan. The milk should rise slightly in the pot.
2. Immediately remove the saucepan from the griddle and add the smoothed custard powder to the hot milk, stirring constantly. Continue stirring until a light bond appears. I always stir for about 2 minutes.
3. Pour the protein powder mixture into the pudding—also with constant stirring—and stir for another 1-2 minutes until everything is smooth.
4. The pudding is now ready and can be eaten hot. If you want to cool it, divide it into individual portions as you need it. This pudding forms "skin" when cooling. If you want to prevent this, put some cling film directly on the hot pudding.

5. Hot, the pudding is viscous comparable to milk soup. Cooled, it is creamy and a little softer than the original. The consistency is ideal for the first few weeks after surgery. Do you want a firmer pudding? Just use a little more custard powder or add a heaped teaspoon of psyllium husks to the finished pudding.

High Protein Pudding - Cinnamon Bun

Cinnamon Roll Pudding or High Protein Pudding "Cinnamon Bun" flavor is one of my favorite variations. This pudding is always warm on the table. So delicious for all cinnamon lovers.

Ingredients:

- 300 ml of milk (1.5%)
- 40 grams of protein powder Birthday Cake flavor (or vanilla, or neutral)
- 20 grams of vanilla custard powder or cream custard powder
- 10 grams of inulin (can be omitted)

For the cinnamon roll cream

- 60 ml of milk
- 20 grams of protein powder birthday cake or similar
- 1 teaspoon of cinnamon
- 1 pinch of salt
- Hot cinnamon bun low carb custard

Preparation:

1. Stir the custard powder with 50 ml of milk and the insulin smooth, set aside protein powder with 50 ml of milk, stir-fry and set aside.
2. Bring the milk to a boil until it rises in the pot. Pull the pot from the hob.

3. While stirring, add the custard powder mixture to the milk and stir vigorously until a firmer pudding is obtained. Continue stirring for at least one minute. (Do not put back on the stove!)
4. Now stir in the protein powder mixture. Depending on the powder type of protein, custard powder may be a firmer pudding. After the Brei phase, this is delicious! The consistency is then comparable to the high protein pudding from the store. In the ripening phase, stir in so much milk that the pudding gets the consistency of yogurt.
5. Divide the pudding into 4 portions.

Cinnamon rolls protein cream

Mix the milk with the protein powder until a smooth cream is produced. Depending on the binding agents in the protein powder, you may need to add a little more liquid. Finally, stir in the cinnamon and the pinch of salt.

You can now inject the cinnamon cream with a piping bag in Cinnamon Bun spiral shape in the pudding.

Secret tip: cream cheese topping

Really American Cinnamon Buns flirt with a cream cheese glaze. Add 30 grams of lean cream cheese with a little milk, add it directly to the cake-flavored pudding, and then put the cinnamon on top. Or below. Delicious and very rich in protein.

High Protein Pudding - Chocolate peanut flavor

Chocolate meets peanut—and love is created. Okay, I have embezzled the caramel. Low Carb caramel is easy to make, but it has a lot of fat, thanks to cream. So it's out of the question. High protein pudding with peanut cream is delicious.

Ingredients:

- Protein Snickers Cream Topping
- 60 ml of milk (1.5%)
- 20 grams of protein powder peanut flavor (or neutral or vanilla ...)
- 10 grams of peanut sauce (no added sugar)
- 1 pinch of salt

For the High Protein Peanut Chocolate Pudding

- 300 ml of milk
- 40 grams of protein powder with peanut flavor
- 20 grams of custard powder chocolate
- 10 grams of inulin (omitting for the first 3 weeks after surgery is optional)
- Snickers pudding recipe

Preparation:

Pudding base recipe

1. For the pudding, mix the custard powder with the inulin with a 50 ml milk and set aside.

2. Mix protein powder with 50 ml of milk to a viscous paste. I take a fork; with a whisk, it goes faster.
3. Bring the milk to a boil until it rises at the top. Pull the pot from the hob.
4. Add the custard powder mixture to the boiled milk with constant stirring and continue stirring for about 2 minutes. The pudding binds, and the first heat goes out a bit.
5. Continue stirring and stir in the protein mixture. I mix the pudding about 2-3 minutes by hand with a whisk. This sucks but brings a nice creamy result, and the protein is well distributed. Attention in the Breiphase: The pudding should have a consistency of yogurt, so it should be relatively fluid. Depending on the protein powder and custard powder variety, it will turn out a little stronger. Just add some milk, so that the consistency is soft if the pudding is more "classic" firmly in the pot.
6. Divide the pudding into four roughly equal portions. If you're cooking for yourself, choose jars with lids.

Prepare protein cream

Mix protein powder and milk for the cream with a mini whisk or with a fork to a uniform cream. Finally, stir in peanut and a pinch of salt.

Now it will be pudding

The peanut cream you simply pour on the individual portions. If you are no longer in the Breiphase, you may like to sprinkle some peanuts and cocoa nibs as a topping. Snickers High Protein Pudding tastes good hot and cold!

MEDITERRANEAN DIET FOR BEGINNERS

Protein pudding vanilla with yogurt cream and tangerines

High Protein Pudding can be made with simple ingredients at home. Instead of cow's milk, lactose-free cow's milk or even almond milk—cashew milk, hazelnut milk, or oat milk can be used. When making your own, you have full control over the type of added sweetness: whether you prefer natural sugar varieties such as coconut blossom sugar or not.

Ingredients:

For the protein pudding

- 300 milliliters of milk
- 40 grams of slightly soluble protein powder
- ½ packet of pudding powder

The sweetness of choice if protein powder is neutral

- 10 grams of inulin (optional)

For the yogurt cream

- 70 grams of Greek yogurt (2% fat)
- 50g of canned mandarins (unsweetened)
- 1 tablespoon of milk
- Protein pudding with mandarin

Preparation:

1. Basic recipe for protein pudding.

2. Smooth the custard powder with 50 ml tablespoons of milk and any added sweetness and set aside. Dissolve protein powder in 50 ml of milk and set aside.

3. Bring remaining milk (200 ml) to a boil in a saucepan.

4. When the milk rises, immediately remove the pot from the plate and add the stirred custard powder-milk mixture to the milk, stirring constantly. The pudding gets a light bond.

5. Continue to stir for about a minute, then add the dissolved protein powder-milk mixture into the hot pudding with constant stirring. When everything is mixed well, the pudding can be divided into 2 portions and eaten either hot or cold.

Protein pudding with yogurt cream

1. Smooth the yogurt with a tablespoon of milk and divide it into 2 portions of pudding. I always place the yogurt in the middle, which makes it look especially nice.

2. Spread canned mandarins (drained) on the protein pudding and dust with cinnamon or vanilla if desired.

Tip in the Breiphase: If your surgery was less than 3 weeks ago, you can mix the canned mandarins with the yogurt vigorously or purée both briefly. But it also tastes great with unsweetened applesauce!

Vanilla Frappuccino

Ingredients:

- 250 ml ready-made vanilla protein shake, frozen in ice cube form
- 60 ml espresso, cold
- 50 ml of milk
- ¼ vanilla pod
- 1 pinch of cinnamon
- 1 pinch of salt

Preparation:

1. Prepare the protein shake according to the preparations. Be sure to use a whey protein or collagen protein without any binder. Very Creamy shakes are only partially suitable for freezing.

Off in the freezer with it

2. Fill the shake into an ice cube mold. Especially suitable form with lid or ice cube bag. The ice cubes freeze for an hour or more, depending on the capacity of your freezer. Use the meantime for cooking the coffee. If you use espresso (Espresso can be a good choice after stomach scaling), you need the extra 50 ml of milk. If you want to make filter coffee, you need more than 100-120 ml to get enough coffee flavor. Then just leave the milk! Let the coffee cool down in peace.

Now it's going to be a Frappuccino!

3. Put the frozen shake ice cubes into the blender together with the ½ vanilla pod, the salt, and the cinnamon.
4. Now add the espresso and the milk or your filter coffee and mix at the highest level with the help of the pestle. The Sößel is a kind of stirrer with which you can stir the mass during the blending. Depending on the model, it is included in the delivery. Stirring is important to prevent the blades from idling and the blender motor flying around your ears.
5. When the mixture looks the same as a Frappuccino, the big portion of Vanilla Frappuccino or Frozen Vanilla Macchiato is ready.
6. This recipe is for the cup size "Venti" designed at Starbucks. If you cannot drink so well, halve the portion size and use only half of the ingredients. The ice cubes stay in the fridge for days—so you can freeze in stock.

CHAPTER 12

BREAKFAST RECIPES

MACKEREL AND EGGS PLATE

A quick and simple keto meal that will keep you satiated for hours.

Prep time: 25 mins

Two servings

Ingredients

- Four eggs
- 2 tbsps. butter, for frying
- 8 oz. canned mackerel with tomato sauce
- 2 oz. lettuce
- ½ red onion
- ¼ cup olive oil
- Salt and pepper

Preparations

1. Fry the eggs in butter the way you prefer, turning them over or without turning them over.
2. Put lettuce, thin slices of red onion, and mackerel on a plate along with the eggs—season to taste. Pour olive oil on top and serve.

Nutrition

Low carb keto

Per portion

Net carbs: 2% (4 g)

Fiber: 1 g

Fat: 77% (59 g)

Protein: 21% (35 g)

kcal: 689

Pancakes with Berries and Whipped Cream

Try these amazing fresh cheese keto pancakes, and you'll never go back to normal pancakes again! Our berry dressing gives you just the right amount of sweetness.

Prep time: 20 mins

Four servings

Ingredients

- Pancakes
- Four eggs
- 7 oz. curd
- 1 tbsp. psyllium shells powder
- 2 oz. butter or coconut oil
- Accompaniment
- 2 oz. fresh raspberries, blueberries or strawberries
- 1 cup whipping cream

Preparations

1. Add the eggs, cottage cheese, and ground psyllium husk powder to a medium bowl and mix. Set aside 5 to 10 minutes to thicken slightly.
2. Heat butter or oil in a nonstick skillet. Fry the pancakes over medium or low heat for 3-4 minutes on each side. Don't make them too big, or they will be difficult to flip.
3. Add whipping cream to a separate bowl and beat until foamy.

4. Serve the pancakes with whipped cream and the berries of your choice.

Advice!

If you want a very fluffy pancake and don't mind spending a little more time making them, you can separate the eggs. Use the yolks as instructed, but beat the whites in a separate bowl. Add the egg whites to the dough, carefully folding them so that the air that entered when whisking them does not escape.

They are also great snacks served cold. Wrap some up and take them to work!

How to store and reheat them:

These pancakes taste better freshly made, but keep well in the refrigerator for 2-3 days. You can also keep them in the freezer for up to three months.

If you want to keep them stacked, it may be best to put a piece of baking paper between each pancake, so they don't stick.

The best way to reheat them is to melt a small piece of butter in a skillet over medium heat and place the pancakes. It only takes about 30 seconds per side to heat them.

Nutrition

Low carb keto

Per portion

Net carbs: 4% (4 g)

Fiber: 3 g

Fat: 83% (39 g)

Protein: 12% (13 g)

kcal: 424

Omelet with Mushrooms

Do you want something quick and easy to start your day? This succulent omelet is very healthy, and it is prepared in the blink of an eye! For the filling, we use fresh mushrooms. Enjoy this keto food for breakfast, lunch, or dinner.

Prep time: 30 mins

One portion

Ingredients

- Three eggs
- 1 oz. butter for frying
- 1 oz. grated cheese
- ¼ yellow onion
- Four large mushrooms
- Salt and pepper

Preparations

1. Break the shells, and apply a pinch of salt and pepper to a cup. Beat them with a fork until smooth and rubbishy.

2. Melt the butter over medium heat, in a frying pan. Attach the mushrooms and onion to the skillet and stir until tender, then add the mixture of eggs around the vegetables.

3. Sprinkle the cheese over the eggs as soon as the omelet begins cooking and is firm but still very raw on top.

4. Using a spatula, take carefully and fold one of the sides of the omelet in half. Remove the pan from the heat when it begins turning golden brown underneath, and slide the omelet onto a tray.

Tip

Serve the omelet with a crispy green salad and served in vinaigrette. Finger-licking good!

Nutrition

Low carb keto

Per portion

Net carbs: 4% (5 g)

Fiber: 1 g

Fat: 76% (44 g)

Protein: 20% (26 g)

kcal: 517

Waffles with Egg, Cheese, and Bacon

These tasty waffles add an extra touch to your breakfast, and they are very easy to prepare! They can be served with poached or fried eggs on top, or you can use them to make sandwiches.

Prep time: 30 mins

Eight servings

Ingredients

- ¼ cup coconut flour
- 1 / 3 cup oat fiber
- 1 / 3 cup isolated unflavored milk protein
- 1½ tsp. baking powder
- ¼ tsp. Salt
- 4 lbs melted butter
- 1 / 3 cup refined coconut oil, melted
- ¼ cup of water
- Four eggs
- ½ tsp. corn extract (optional)
- ½ cup cheddar cheese
- Two chopped chives
- 4 oz. chopped cooked bacon

Preparations

1. Prepare the waffle iron according to the manufacturer's Preparations.
2. Mix all the dry ingredients. Add the melted butter, coconut oil, eggs, and water. Whisk with a hand mixer. Add the corn extract, the cheese, the chives, and the bacon.

3. With a spoon, incorporate the dough into the waffle iron, taking care that it does not overflow on the sides. Cook until waffles are golden brown and slightly crisp. Serve hot.

Advice!

Casein and lactose are removed from whey isolate and is not the same as whey protein, which can be very insulin genic. Check the ingredients of the isolated whey protein to make sure it doesn't have any added sweeteners. Some good brands without any carbohydrates are Isopure, Jay Robb, or Hoosier Farm.

In addition to breakfast, these waffles are great for brunch, lunch, or dinner. Try serving them with minced pork, bacon, beef brisket, or even as a garnish with a good soup.

Leftovers can be kept for up to four days. They can also be frozen and heated in a toaster, hot skillet, or oven at 350 °F (180 °C).

Nutrition

Low carb keto
Per portion
Net carbs: 0% (1 g)
Fiber: 5 g
Fat: 97% (204 g)
Protein: 3% (12 g)
kcal: 1855

Coconut Porridge

Have you got up wanting some warm cereal? Well, enjoy this satisfying, warm, and comforting keto delight. Happiness in a bowl!

Prep time: 40 mins

Two portions

Ingredients

- One beaten egg
- 1 tbsp. coconut flour
- One pinch psyllium husks powder
- One pinch of salt
- 1 oz. butter or coconut oil
- 4 tbsps. coconut cream

Preparations

1. In a small bowl, combine the egg, coconut flour, psyllium husk powder, and salt.
2. Melt the butter and coconut cream over low heat. Add to the egg mixture, beating slowly until obtaining a thick and creamy texture.
3. Serve with coconut milk or cream. Put some fresh or frozen berries on top and enjoy!

Advice!

If you have leftover coconut milk, you can use it for a smoothie. It will thicken it a little, it will be richer, and it will satisfy you more.

Nutrition

Low carb keto

Per portion

Net carbs: 3% (4 g)

Fiber: 5 g

Fat: 89% (49 g)

Protein: 8% (9 g)

kcal: 486

Low carb pancakes

These light crepes are perfect for breakfast, brunch, or dessert. Add a few berries and whipped cream to get a keto delight that the whole family can enjoy.

Prep time: 20 mins

Four servings

Ingredients

- Eight eggs
- Two cups whipping cream
- ½ cup water
- ¼ tsp. Salt
- 2 tbsps. psyllium shells powder
- 3 oz. Butter

Preparations

1. In a bowl, mix the eggs, cream, water, and salt with a hand mixer.
2. Gradually incorporate the psyllium husk powder while continuing to beat until you get a uniform dough. Reserve for at least 10 minutes.
3. Fry in butter like normal pancakes. You should use one dl (½ cup) for each crepe. Make sure that the pan is not too big or too hot, keep it at medium-high temperature. Don't get impatient, but wait until the top is almost dry before turning them over.

Some tips!

- Start by frying a small crepe to see if the dough is holding tightly together. There are differences between brands of psyllium husk powder, and even the size of the eggs can affect the result. If the dough is too thick, you can reduce it with a little cream, milk or water; if it is too dilute, add more psyllium husk powder.
- You can serve the pancakes with whipping cream and the berries you prefer.

Nutrition

Low carb keto

Per portion

Net carbs: 2% (4 g)

Fiber: 3 g

Fat: 89% (68 g)

Protein: 9% (15 g)

kcal: 686

Breakfast tapas

If you are looking for a delicious dish to serve multiple people, look no further! If you use good quality cheese, cold cuts, and nuts, you will have an exquisite keto feast in no time, and it is fresh, colorful, and tasty.

Prep time: 25 mins

Six servings

Ingredients

- 4 oz. cheddar cheese
- 8 oz. cured ham
- 8 oz. chorizo
- ½ cup mayonnaise
- 4 oz. cucumbers
- 2 oz. Red peppers

Preparations

1. Cut the cold cuts, cheese, and vegetables into slices, sticks or cubes.
2. Plating, serving, and enjoying.

Some tips!

Don't wait to have guests at home! This ingenious dish is so easy and fast that you can enjoy it at any time.

You can use different cheeses, such as mozzarella, manchego, gouda, etc., and different cold cuts such as serrano ham or salami.

If you want to add a little more flavor and color, add some avocado, mozzarella, or radishes and walnuts. But be sure to adjust the grams of carb, fat, and protein-based on the changes you make.

Nutrition

Low carb keto

Per portion

Net carbs: 2% (4 g)

Fiber: 0 g

Fat: 77% (56 g)

Protein: 20% (33 g)

kcal: 664

Boiled eggs with mayonnaise

Egg lovers gather together! This recipe is so simple, so tasty... And it is exactly what your body needs to be satiated. Combine them with ripe avocado and our homemade mayonnaise recipe, and you'll have a delicious keto dish instantly.

Prep time: 15 mins

Four servings

Ingredients

- Eight eggs
- 8 tbsps. Mayonnaise
- Avocado (optional)

Preparations

1. Bring water to a boil in a pot.
2. Optional: Make small holes in the eggs using an egg puncher.
3. Carefully place the eggs in the water.
4. Boil the eggs for 5–6 minutes so that they are gone through water, 6–8 minutes for medium level, and 8-10 minutes so that they are very hard.
5. Serve with mayonnaise.

Nutrition

Low carb keto
Per portion
Net carbs: 1% (1 g)
Fiber: 0 g
Fat: 84% (29 g)
Protein: 15% (11 g)
kcal:

Benedictine eggs on an avocado bed

A classic brunch. This time converted to keto, replacing the traditional English muffin with a bed of avocado. Poached eggs, smoked salmon, and Hollandaise is still there, but without any carb. A new healthy version with a great taste.

Prep time: 15 mins

Four servings

Ingredients

- Hollandaise sauce
- Three egg yolks
- 1 tbsp. lemon juice
- salt and pepper to taste
- 8½ tbsps. Butter
- Benedictine eggs
- Two avocados pitted and skinless
- Four eggs
- 5 oz. smoked salmon

Preparations

1. Take a jar or any microwaveable jar that fits the mixer. Put the butter inside and melt it in the microwave for about 20 seconds.
2. Add the egg yolks and lemon juice to the butter. Place the mixer in the bottom of the jar and beat until a creamy white layer is formed. Then carefully raise and lower the mixer to create a creamy white layer—season to taste.

3. Place a pan with water on the fire and bring to a boil. Reduce heat to medium-low.
4. Add the eggs one by one to a measuring bowl, then carefully add them to the water. Stirring the water in circles will create a small eddy that will prevent the egg white from separating too far from the yolks. Cook them for 3-4 minutes, depending on the consistency you want the yolks to have. Remove the poached eggs with a slotted spoon and place them on kitchen paper to absorb the excess water.
5. Cut the avocados in half and remove the seeds and skin. Cut the base of each half so that they remain firm on the plate. Top each with a little smoked salmon, one egg, and garnish with a generous tablespoon of Hollandaise sauce.
6. They must be eaten on the spot, and they cannot be saved or reheated. Hollandaise sauce can be stored in a jar in the refrigerator for up to 4 days.

Some tips!

You can use an egg poach. You just need to grease the molds with butter before putting an egg in each mold.

Another method of keeping the whites firm and preventing them from separating is to add a pinch of vinegar or a few drops of lemon to the boiling water.

You will get a fantastic presentation if you sprinkle some paprika on top or decorate them with parsley.

Nutrition

Low carb keto

Per portion

Net carbs: 2% (3 g)

Fiber: 7 g

Fat: 85% (47 g)

Protein: 13% (16 g)

kcal: 514

Scrambled eggs with basil and butter

An original and simple, yet elegant version of a classic breakfast: scrambled eggs with cream cheese, fresh herbs and butter! Start the day with these delicious eggs and the right touch of basil. They are creamy, juicy, and full of cheese. They will leave you so satiated that you can delay lunch!

Prep time: 25 mins

Four portions

Ingredients

- 2 tbsps. Butter
- Two eggs
- 2 tbsps. whipping cream
- salt and ground black pepper
- 2 oz. grated cheese
- 2 tbsps. fresh basil

Preparations

1. Melt the butter in a frying pan over low heat.
2. Add the eggs, cream, cheese, and dressing to a small bowl. Whisk lightly and add to the pan.
3. Stir with a spatula from the edges to the center until the eggs have been stirred. If you prefer them soft and creamy, stir at a low temperature until they reach the consistency you want.
4. Finish by sprinkling the basil on top.

Nutrition

Low carb keto

Per portion

Net carbs: 2% (3 g)

Fiber: 0 g

Fat: 82% (58 g)

Protein: 16% (26 g)

kcal: 634

Cupcakes eggs to go

Here's an inspiring way to make eggs to go! With so many ways to make eggs, this one adds to the fun with creative optional filling options. It's keto and egg-Celente!

Prep time: 20 mins

Six servings

Ingredients

- 12 eggs
- Salt and ground black pepper to taste
- 4 oz. cooked bacon

Preparations

1. Preheat oven to 200 °C (400 °F).
2. Place the paper cake molds in the muffin tin. Eggs adhere easily even on non-stick surfaces, except for silicon ones.
3. Break an egg in each space and add the filling of your choice. Choose one of our fillers below or invent yours! We will make the classic minced bacon.
4. Season to taste.
5. Bake for about 15 minutes or until eggs is done.

Advice!

When making a filling, your imagination is the only limit. Regardless of your choice, you can increase the fat ratio by adding grated cheese, mayonnaise, or sour cream before baking.

Other suggestions for fillings are ham, turkey, salami, all kinds of cheeses: chili peppers, Parmesan cheese, blue cheese, etc., in addition to avocado, cocktail tomatoes, chopped onion, minced garlic, and jalapeños/fresh or pickled chili. Experiment and have fun!

Nutrition

Low carb keto

Per portion

Net carbs: 2% (1 g)

Fiber: 0 g

Fat: 71% (16 g)

Protein: 27% (13 g)

kcal: 205

Fried eggs with kale and pork

Present something delicious! Eggs and vegetables, along with crispy walnuts and crispy pork, give you great texture and flavor. Create this butter-filled keto wonder in a single skillet any night of the week!

Prep time: 35 mins

Four servings

Ingredients

- ½ lb kale
- 3 oz. Butter
- 6 oz. smoked pork belly or bacon
- ¼ cup frozen cranberries
- 1 oz. pecans or walnuts
- Four eggs
- Salt and pepper

Preparations

1. Cut and chop the kale into large squares (pre-washed kale is an excellent shortcut). Melt two-thirds of the butter in a skillet and fry the kale quickly over high heat until lightly browned around the edges.
2. Remove the kale from the pan and set aside. Brown the bacon or pork bacon in the same skillet until crisp.
3. Lower the fire. Put the sautéed kale back in the pan and add the blueberries and

walnuts. Stir until heated through—Reserve in a bowl.

4. Turn up the heat and fry the eggs in the rest of the butter. Season to taste. Plate two fried eggs with each serving of vegetables and serve immediately.

Advice!

Use other vegetables... cabbage, chard, or spinach are tasty variations. Or make it a garnish by removing the fried eggs.

Nutrition

Low carb keto

Per portion

Net carbs: 3% (8 g)

Fiber: 6 g

Fat: 87% (99 g)

Protein: 10% (26 g)

kcal: 1032

Iced tea

A very fresh and refreshing iced tea... Quench your thirst so much that you won't miss the sugar! Enjoy the taste of summer all year round with this classic low carb drink. Do it for everyone!

Preparation time: 10m

Two servings

Ingredients

- 2 cups cold water
- One tea bag
- 1 cup of ice cubes
- Flavorings of your choice, such as sliced lemon or fresh mint

Preparations

1. Combine the tea, flavoring, and half the cold water in a jug and leave it in the refrigerator for 1-2 hours.
2. Remove the teabag and flavoring. You can replace it with a fresh new flavor if you want.
3. Add the rest of the cold water and serve with many ice cubes. One of the simple pleasures in life!

Some tips!

Try it with any type of tea you like: green, white, jasmine or black. You can add a couple of slices of peach, orange, lemon, or lime or some mint leaves to give it a great flavor. The possibilities are endless, and any fruit will do just fine!

Nutrition

Low carb keto

Per portion

Net carbs: 0% (0 g)

Fiber: 0 g

Fat: 0% (0 g)

Protein: 0% (0 g)

kcal: 0

LUNCH RECIPES

Creamy Risotto with White Meat, Mushrooms, And Vegetables

Servings: 4 servings

Prep Time: 1hr

A great risotto to enjoy. Lots of flavors, a little spice.

Note: everything is in the mix. Frequent stirring is just what it takes to make the risotto very creamy (not sticky from rice but creamy).

Ingredients:

- ½ kg of chicken breast
- Two tablespoons olive oil
- Four DCL rice
- One young onion link
- Two medium carrots
- 5-6 larger mushrooms
- Two teaspoons of butter (so measure unheated)
- 1.5 l prepared chicken cube soup (you may not be able to use everything but have it ready)
- ½ teaspoon salt
- ¼ teaspoon pepper

Preparation:

1. Prepare the meat—wash it with cold water and remove the pieces of fat and what is already excess. Cut the meat into cubes. Also, prepare the vegetables so you can focus on stirring the risotto later. Divide the onions into white and green. Cut both pieces into cubes, but keep them separate.

2. Also, clean the carrots and cut them into small cubes. Wash the mushrooms well, clean them (I peel the surface, most do not do this, it is not obligatory), then cut them into pieces, the stem into 2-3 parts, the cap in half, and into some six parts (if nice, large). They should feel when they bite, and they should not be thin pieces.

3. Whisk the soup cubes into 1.5 liters of water (depending on how much water the cube is, it depends on how many soup cubes you use) and boil to get soup.

4. Now you start preparing. On olive oil and over medium heat, fry the white meat to give it full color and soften. Stir to keep it from reaching the bottom. After about 10 minutes, add the mushrooms and stir. Both meat and mushrooms will release their juice. Continue until all the liquid has boiled.

5. When boiling the meat and mushrooms, add the garlic. Add the carrot too. Altogether, fry until the vegetables soften, stirring further until they are caught in the bottom.

6. When the vegetables seem to have softened, add the butter (I had none, so the margarine was served) and stir until melted.
7. Now add the rice. Fry it all together just until the rice has a little color (be careful not to burn, stir constantly and let it be a little weaker fire).
8. Start adding soup. Add just enough to make the rice barely liquid. Stir frequently. When the soup is cooked into the rice, add some more soup and stir again until the rice appears to be cooked.
9. Rice should not be overcooked, but neither should it be tough. Take some and try. When you don't feel the crispness, that's about it.
10. You will consume most of the prepared soup, but don't make the risotto thick or too sparse.
11. Finally, add the green portion of the young onion, stir it all together on the heat for a minute—two, and your risotto is ready. Serve it if you like—well worth it, it gives a great extra flavor, with grated cheese on top (edamer or the like). Yes, serve it now, don't wait for it to cool...

Enjoy it!

Beef stew with homemade pasta

Servings: for eight people

Time: 30 minutes of preparation, 3-4 hours of light crunching

Ingredients for stew:

- 2 kg of shoulder beef meat
- 1/2 kg of onion
- about one DCL of oil
- 2 l tomato juice (I suggest Tomatillo)
- Three DCL of red wine
- Five teaspoons sugar (should try, should sweeten but not sweet)
- Two teaspoons of salt (should try, not tasteless, but not too salty)
- One teaspoon ground pepper
- One teaspoon of oregano
- About two teaspoons of dried basil (But this is the amount for a large, whole dried basil, not crushed. Fine—about 2-3 teaspoons)

And more:

- 200 g Trappist
- Homemade pasta made from 6 eggs and 600 g flour (or two packs of 400 g each)

Preparation:

1. Cut the onion into cubes or grind it in a bowl, but it will not become porridge. In a large, deep saucepan, fry the onion with oil.

When the onions have become translucent, add the cut beef to the cubes. Whisk the beef in the oil until it is colored on all sides and until it has released its juice. Do not add water. It would be necessary to fry the meat in several rounds to get the "crust" and to keep all the juices inside and thus be juicy. I didn't do it, but I distilled it in my juice.

2. When the meat has received color on all sides and has released a lot of liquid, pour the tomatoes on the meat. Add the spices, adding half the amount of sugar and salt, not all at once. Leave the red wine for later. Leave it all so that it cuts the clock - an hour and a half. Now is the time to knead the dough and put it in the fridge.

3. After this time, add the red wine and let the meat crunch with the wine for 10 minutes. Then try the softness a little. Add the sugar and salt to it as I stated in the ingredients, it should sweeten but not sweet, and tasty but not salty.

4. Allow the meat to crunch further, the menu has been crunching for a total of about 4 hours, but at a completely lightweight (1.5 - 2 in the range of 9). Also, you can now move on to developing the test. Grind the meat until you have cooked the pasta, only remove it from the cooker when ready to serve, nothing bothers it.

5. On the cooked pasta, grate the cheese if you like, serve it in a plate. Pour the meat over the pasta with plenty of oil. Enjoy!

Pea stew with white meat, carrots, and dumplings

Servings: for four people

Prep Time: 1 h 30 minutes

Ingredients:

- 500-600 g chicken breast
- One large onion
- 1/2 DCL of onion water
- 8 - 10 medium-sized potatoes
- Four large carrots
- One can of 400 g peas
- 2 l of water
- Two tablespoons red ground peppers
- 3 + 1 teaspoon of seasoning (maybe homemade or, for example, Aleva culminate natur)
- 1/3 teaspoon fresh ground pepper (maybe more, maybe less)
- One teaspoon dried parsley leaf
- 1/2 teaspoon dried basil
  Ingredients for dumplings:
- Two eggs
- A good pinch of salt
- About seven tablespoons of flour

Preparation:

1. Wash white meat under cold water. Remove any excess grease. Cut the meat into cubes. In a large non-stick frying pan (e.g., a stone-

coated one would be great) dinstate (steaming, as it is rightly said) in your meat juice, to get a white color on all sides. Allow it to simmer a little without adding water, oil, anything...

2. While the meat is steaming, clean the potatoes, carrots, onions. Wash everything well. Cut the potatoes into cubes, carrots into half-rolls about 1/2 cm wide. Cut the onion into small cubes. Put the carrots and potatoes in a larger pan to cook the stew.

3. Transfer the sliced meat to potatoes and carrots. Put the onion in a frying pan and fry it without adding water or oil to the same frying pan in which you grilled the meat. When the onion has softened a little, pour it over with 1/2 dcl of water, and let it simmer in the water for a little while. Transfer the onions to the meat and other vegetables.

4. Pour 2 liters of hot water over meat and vegetables. Add red pepper, three teaspoons of seasoning, pepper, parsley, and basil. Leave it to boil, reduce the volume of the roast to crunch the peppers and cover. Cook until the potatoes are almost crumbled.

5. Twenty minutes before the end of cooking, add the peas from the can. Do not strain it, do not rinse it, just press it with a spoon when removing it from the can, then straight into the stew. This will give the peas a bit of a sweet taste to the stew, generally, an extra-fine taste...

Preparing dumplings:

6. Prepare mixture for dumplings. Break two eggs, add salt, and whisk well. For starters, add some five tablespoons of flour and whisk well with a fork. The mixture should be such that you can grab a teaspoon without leaking it. So, while it is not, gradually add more flour. Whisk it not to be lumpy.

7. Put the dumplings in the stew. Dip a teaspoon (the best ones are small but long) to dip in the stew, and then grab the dumplings mixture (about half a teaspoon). Dip the teaspoon again into the stew until the mixture falls into the shaft. Allow the dumplings to cook for about 10 minutes.

Fast melters with fried eggs and various vegetables

Servings: 2-4 people

Prep Time: 30 minutes

Ingredients:

- 400 g of tagliatelle (long, thick noodles)
- 2-3 tablespoons of oil
- Three red peppers
- One zucchini
- Two onions
- Three tomatoes
- Three eggs
- One teaspoon salt
- One teaspoon basil
- One teaspoon of oregano
- ½ teaspoon freshly ground pepper

Preparation:

1. Feel free to immediately place a large pan full of water to boil, add a teaspoon of salt to it. If you boil the water and you are not very happy with how you progress with the vegetables, just reduce it to a unit, it will be easy to step up afterward without waiting for the dough...

2. Peel the pepper from the seeds, wash it and chop it into larger cubes. Also, peel the onion, wash it, and cut it into lobes. Peel the squash and cut into cubes. Wash the tomatoes well, halve and cut into cubes.

3. Place the oil in a large frying pan to heat it, turn the hot pan over to medium strength. Add the onion oil to the warmed oil, just fry it a little (don't have to wait until it's softened) and immediately add the peppers as well as the squash. Fry the vegetables on medium-strength broth to soften (not very much).

4. Afterward, add the tomatoes to the onions, peppers, and squash. When you add the tomatoes, boost the roast to about 2/3 of the strength (not to burn) so that the vegetables are fried as soon as the tomatoes release the juice, so that the juice should evaporate. When all the tomato liquid has evaporated, add the spices and remove the pan from the ring. By the way, boil the melts in boiling water...

5. In the second pan, fry three eggs (mixed with two pinches of salt and a little pepper, just on top of the knife) over a little oil (1 tablespoon). It doesn't have to be a dry egg. Add the fried egg to the vegetables, then combine everything.

6. When the vegetables with the eggs are ready, add the cooked melters to the vegetables, stirring gently (maybe with two forks or similar), making sure the dough does not crumble. When you have added all the pasta to the vegetables, return the pan to medium strength, and fry for a minute, stirring constantly.

Have a nice time, and enjoy your lunch!

Ground stew in red wine, tomatoes, with various vegetables

Servings: 8 people

Time:2 hours

Before you start cooking, please note:

It is not advisable to add water as the stew does not need to be "watery." Adding water will make you lose the flavor of the tomatoes in the dish, which would be a shame. I added 2-3 small cups of water, but only because the potatoes were just weird and cooked for a long time and didn't even decompose in the end... so that not all the liquid from the stew boils until the potatoes are cooked...

Ingredients:

- One DCL of oil
- Three onions
- One pepper (green or red)
- 700 g of minced pork
- Five larger tomatoes
- One larger flask
- Ten medium sized potatoes
- 2 l Tomatello Juice Tomato
- Three DCL of red wine
- Two packs of frozen vegetable stew (carrots, peas, green beans, potatoes)
- Five teaspoons sugar
- Two flat teaspoons of pepper

- 3 - 4 teaspoons salt (should not be salty, but add gradually, repeatedly)
- Two teaspoons of dried oregano
- Two tablespoons of dried basil (if more dried, almost whole leaves, and if small, three teaspoons)

Preparation:

1. Before cooking, prepare all vegetables (except frozen, you do not need to defrost it).
2. Cut the onions into cubes, pepper the seeds, and cut into smaller strips, 1-2cm long. Wash the tomatoes, cut into cubes. Cut the petioles, peel them off the peel, and cut into cubes. Also, peel and chop the potatoes. Put them in cold water until it turns black.
3. Heat the oil in a kettle. Add onions, leave to soften, add peppers, also allow to fry until softened halfway through. Stir vegetables to keep them from burning. On the softened vegetables, add the minced meat, stir and fry until it is colored on all sides. After that, fry it for another 10 minutes. Work everything at a moderate fire rate.
4. When your meat is fried, add the tomatoes, followed by the zucchini. Let it crumble, without adding any liquid, until the tomatoes have released their juice. Stir occasionally. When the tomatoes release the juice, add the potatoes, tomato juice, and all the spices (salt not all at once).

5. Allow the dish to crunch and add the red wine after 15 minutes. Cook the stew further until the potatoes are almost completely softened. Twenty minutes before the end of cooking, add the frozen vegetables and let the stew simmer until all the vegetables are cooked through. It should not decompose but soften.

Pasta with feta cheese and fried bacon - Túrós csusza variant

Servings: 4 people

Time: 30 minutes

Ingredients:

- 400 g thick pasta
- 200 g sour cream
- 300 g feta sira
- 300 g of bacon

Preparation:

1. Pour water into a large saucepan, add some salt and allow water to boil. If you have learned, you can add some oil, though, the essence is in cooking the dough without sticking it, in bubbles. That is, the water is constantly boiling well while the dough is cooking, the oil does not matter, because it certainly floats on the surface...
2. While the water is boiling, chop the bacon into small cubes and place it in the pan to fry. You do not need any extra fat. Stir the bacon from time to time, so you don't get caught in the bottom. Remove the fried bacon on a napkin to absorb excess fat.
3. Put the dough in boiling water to cook. Do not overcook it, so it does not fall apart and become sticky. Drain, rinse with cold water and place in a larger bowl. Add the sour cream to the dough, and mix. Then crush the

feta cheese on the pasta, then stir. You've got the basics.

4. Serve the dough in plates. Only then, sprinkle the dough with the fried bacon so that everything on the plate is mixed into the dough. If you immediately mix it into all the dough, the fried bacon will soften and lose what's best in the whole story - its crispness.

Have fun, and enjoy it!

DINNER RECIPES

Wholegrain Pancake with Chicken

Prep time: 35 mins

4 servings

Ingredients

- Chicken breast - 120g
- Wholemeal pancake - 65g
- Skyr - 30g
- Salt
- Black pepper
- Rosemary
- Sweet pepper
- Garlic powder
- Crushed rasca
- Olive oil
- Oregano
- Garlic - 2 cloves
- Tomato - 30g
- Iceberg lettuce - 20g
- Onion - 15g

Preparation

1. Cut the chicken breast into thin slices or noodles.
2. Salt and season on both sides.
3. Roast vigorously on a little oil.

4. While roasting chicken breasts, create a dressing by mixing a scissor with crushed garlic, a little salt, and black pepper.
5. We make the spice for "kebab" by mixing 3/4 tsp. salt, 3 tsps. sweet pepper, ½ tart oregano, one tart garlic powder, one tart rosemary, and one tart crushed raspberry.
6. When the chicken breasts are ready, set them aside, and heat the whole meal pancake in a clean pan.
7. Sprinkle the warm pancake with garlic dressing, add chopped vegetables, meat, and season with spices (quantity according to your taste).

Radish Pasta with Chicken

Prep time: 45 mins

2 servings

Ingredient

- White radish - 130g
- Chicken breast - 100g
- Peas - 30g
- Ground red pepper
- Salt
- Oil - 1pl
- Soy sauce - 2pl

Preparation

1. Clean the white radish and prepare pasta with a special scraper or grinder.
2. Put in a pan and cook over low heat for about 5 minutes. Be careful not to sinter the pasta.
3. Season with soy sauce.
4. Cut the chicken breasts into small pieces.
5. Add salt and roast to a little oil according to your preference.
6. Mix the finished chicken breasts with the pasta, heat, and add a little red pepper.

Avocado Salad with Ham, Cheese, and Egg

Prep time: 55 mins

2 servings

Ingredients

- Edam 30% - 60g
- Chicken ham - 150g
- Eggs - 2pcs
- Avocado - 1pc
- Tomato - 1pc
- Salt
- Iceberg lettuce - 40g

Preparation

1. Boil the eggs softly (approximately 8-10 minutes).
2. While the eggs are boiling, cut the chicken ham, Edam, and tomato into small pieces.
3. Add avocado crushed with a fork to the vegetables.
4. Mix well and add the torn iceberg lettuce.
5. Mix with soft-boiled eggs and season with salt as needed.

Tuna Salad with Cottage Cheese

Prep time: 15 mins

2 servings

Ingredients

- Tuna in its juice - 150g
- Low-fat lump curd - 100g
- Tomato - 30g
- Capers - 30g
- Onion - 20g
- Edam - 20g
- Chive
- Butter - 20g

Preparation

1. Mix tuna with cottage cheese and a little slightly melted butter.
2. Add the chopped onion, capers, tomatoes, and chives.
3. Season with finely grated Edam.
4. Let stand for 5 minutes.

Turkey Cuts with Cottage Cheese Salad

Prep time: 30 mins

4 servings

Ingredient

- Turkey breast - 200g
- Low-fat lump curd - 100g
- Tomato - 30g
- Capers - 30g
- Onion - 20g
- Edam - 20g
- Chive
- Black pepper
- Salt
- Eggs - 1pc
- Spelled whole meal flour
- Butter - 20g

Preparation

1. Cut the turkey breasts into slices.
2. Salt and season on both sides, press the pepper and salt into the cuttings.
3. Wrap in spelled flour, egg, and again in spelled flour.
4. Roast on low heat without using oil (watch out for low heat so that the flour does not burn and the crunchy cover is preserved).
5. When the cuts are roasted on both sides, add a little butter and roast on both sides to make the wrapper baked.

6. We prepare the salad by mixing cottage cheese, chopped onion, chives, tomatoes, and capers.
Season with a little room temperature butter and finely grated Edam.

Baked Turkey Breast with Ham And Cheese

Prep time: 35 mins

4 servings

Ingredients

- Turkey Breast - 300g
- Edam - 40g
- Chicken Ham 90% - 20g
- Butter - 20g
- Oriental Vegetable Mixture - 300g
- Salt
- Black Pepper
- Soy Sauce - 2pl
- Spelled Flour

Preparation

1. Cut the turkey breast into slices.
2. Season with salt and pepper.
3. Wrap in spelled flour.
4. Roast in a pan without using oil for about 10 minutes on each side until the turkey breast is ready.
5. Place slices of ham and grated cheese on the turkey breast and finally pieces of butter.
6. Cover with a lid and cook until the cheese melts.
7. Without a lid, let the turkey breast lightly fry the buttercup and set aside.
8. Let the oriental vegetable mixture melt in a pan.

9. When the mixture is melted, and the water is almost all evaporated, add the soy sauce.
10. Cook for 10 minutes with continuous stirring.
11. Turkey breast is served with a mixture of vegetables.

Natural Turkey Breast with Grilled Carrots

Prep time: 50 mins

2 servings

Ingredients

- Turkey breast - 200g
- Carrot - 150g
- Salt
- Black pepper
- Thyme
- Oregano
- Garlic pepper

Preparation

1. Salt and season the turkey breasts. Let stand for 5 minutes.
2. Roast on a wok without using oil.
3. Meanwhile, clean the carrots and cut in half.
4. When the turkey breasts are fried, we set them aside.
5. Clean the wok and add the carrots, which we season with thyme, salt, and garlic pepper.
6. Grill for about 10 minutes on each side over low heat.

Cheese Salad With Onion

Prep time: 25 mins

1 serving

Ingredients

- Lump curd - 200g
- Butter - 30g
- Salt
- Onion - 50g
- Eggs - 2pcs
- Grating cheese - 50g

Preparation

1. Mix lump curd with butter to a fine consistency.
2. Boil the eggs softly and mix.
3. Mix with grated cheese and finely chopped onion.
4. Finally, season with salt.

Turkey Steak with Cranberry Sauce

Prep time: 50 mins

2 servings

Ingredients

- Turkey cutlets - 130g
- Rice - 80g
- Turmeric
- Salt
- Black pepper
- Rosemary
- Sunflower oil - 4pl
- Butter - 5g
- Chives - 10g
- Cranberry sauce - 20g

Preparation

1. Heat the oil in a pan.
2. Insert a turkey cutlet, which we seasoned with black pepper, salt, and thyme on both sides.
3. Roast on each side as needed - about 10 minutes.
4. After roasting, suck all the oil from the meat with kitchen towels.
5. Boil the rice in approximately 200 - 250 ml of salt-flavored water.
6. Mix cooked rice with a little turmeric and butter and chopped chives.
7. Serve with cranberry sauce.

Egg Salad with Ham And Cheese

Prep time: 30 mins

2 servings

Ingredients

- Eggs - 5pcs
- Turkey ham - 200g
- Hood - 1pc
- Tomatoes - 2pcs
- Edam - 100g
- Chive
- White yogurt - 140g

Preparation

1. Boil the eggs half-hard for 8-10 minutes.
2. Clean it from the shell, cut it in half first, and then cut it into smaller pieces.
3. Cut the hood, tomatoes, and turkey ham into small pieces.
4. Mix with chopped chives, white yogurt, eggs, and grated Edam cheese.

Baked Zucchini with Mozzarella

Prep time: 35 mins

2 servings

Ingredients

- Zucchini - 150g
- English bacon - 100g
- Mozzarella - 100g
- Chive

Preparation

1. Cut English bacon into medium-sized pieces.
2. Fry lightly in a pan.
3. Toast the zucchini wheels on both sides.
4. So far, grate the mozzarella.
5. Place the fried bacon on top of the zucchini wheels.
6. Sprinkle with mozzarella and sliced chives.

Zucchini Mixture with Mushrooms and Chicken

Prep time: 35 mins

3 servings

Ingredients

- Zucchini - 100g
- Champions - 50g
- Chicken breast - 100g
- Carrot - 50g
- Mozzarella - 10g
- Salt
- Sunflower oil - 2pl
- Garlic - 2 cloves

Preparation

1. Cut the chicken breasts into smaller pieces and fry in 1pl of warmed sunflower oil. Season with salt while roasting.
2. Meanwhile, clean the champions and cut them into slices. Put in a separate bowl.
3. Continue to clean zucchini and carrots.
4. Cut the zucchini into smaller pieces, grate the carrots.
5. Put the roasted chicken breasts and the champions on the pan.
6. If necessary, we can add a few drops of oil.
7. Roast the mushrooms evenly on both sides together with the garlic cut into pieces.

8. Add zucchini and grated carrots to the roasted shamans.
9. Cook together for 10 minutes.
10. Add chicken breast and cook for 5 minutes.
11. Serve with grated mozzarella.

Low - Carbohydrate Pasta with Turkey Meat

Prep time: 35 mins

4 servings

Ingredient

- Low-fat cream cheese - 200g
- Eggs - 4pcs
- Turkey breast - 100g
- Delicious onion
- Tomato
- Sesame seeds
- Full mustard - 2pl
- Soy sauce - 1pl
- Olive oil
- Solamyl

Preparation

1. Beat one egg, add whole mustard, sesame seeds, soy sauce, olive oil, and Solamyl.
2. Mix thoroughly until a marinade is formed.
3. Put sliced turkey breast in the marinade and let stand for at least 30 minutes.
4. Roast turkey meat in a Teflon pan without oil (it is already in the marinade).
5. Prepare the dough for low-carbohydrate pasta by mixing scrambled eggs (3 pcs) and low-fat cream cheese.
6. Place the dough on a baking sheet lined with baking paper and spread in a medium-thick layer.

7. Bake for twenty minutes in an oven heated to 200 °C.
8. When the "pasta" is almost baked (they start to catch color), cut the dough into pieces and continue baking.
9. When preparing low-carbohydrate pasta, it may seem to you during baking that the pasta will not stick together. But be patient and wait until they are baked.

Red Cabbage Salad with Carrots

Prep time: 15 mins

2 servings

Ingredients

- Carrots - 80g
- Red cabbage - 80g
- Red onion - 30g
- Whole mustard - 30g
- Eggs - 1pc
- Green onion - 30g

Preparation

1. Cut carrots and red cabbage into thin strips.
2. Add the red onion cut into small pieces.
3. Wash the green onion and finely chop the green part.
4. Mix the ingredients and taste with full-fat mustard, salt, and spices as needed.
5. Serve with a roasted egg (without oil).

Chicken Salad of Red Cabbage

Prep time: 25 mins

2 servings

Ingredients

- Red cabbage - 80g
- Carrot - 60g
- Red onion - 30g
- Chicken breast - 200g
- Butter - 5g
- Spices on china
- White yogurt - 35g
- BIO chicken broth - 1 / 2pcs

Preparation

1. Fry the chicken in melted butter.
2. Season with crushed chicken broth and spice for china.
3. Meanwhile, clean the vegetables and cut them into small pieces.
4. Set the carrots aside.
5. After roasting the chicken breasts, simmer the carrots until soft.
6. All ingredients are mixed with yogurt and served.

CHAPTER 13

MAIN DISHES

35. Feta Tomato Casserole With Bacon

Ingredients

- 150 grams of feta cheese, reduced in fat (9%)
- 30 grams of bacon
- 4 cocktail tomatoes
- 1.5 ml of olive oil
- 20 grams of grated cheese

You can choose spices and herbs to sprinkle.

Notes on the fat level:

I always take with Bacon the reduced-fat feta cheese because otherwise, the total amount of fat in the meal is too high. This is not "harmful"—I just cannot stand it. Decide for yourself which fat level you prefer.

Notes portion size:

The portion is for a casserole. This is enough for someone with a normal stomach for a meal; for me, it depends on the daily form 1.5 - 2 portions.

Preparation:

1. Preheat the oven to 200 degrees and rub a small, refractory shape with a little olive oil.
2. Place the drained feta in the bowl, sprinkle the bacon over it, put the tomatoes in, put the cheese on it, and put it in the oven with it!
3. After about 20-25 minutes, the grated cheese is golden yellow; your Bacon Feta casserole is then ready to enjoy.

36. Rouxdolph's Banana Peanut Burger

This is one of the best burger recipes in the world - a real favorite food. If you like the roasting aromas of beef, peanut sauce, chili, and a hint of the creamy sweetness of the banana, this is the one for you.

The burger recipe is also extremely simple and is on the table in 10 minutes. Here I propose the preparation in the pan—the Banana Peanut Burger recipe without rolls is also one of the best burger recipes in the world when it comes to cooking on the grill.

Ingredients

- A few salad leaves as decoration
- 100 grams of raw beef tartar
- ½ small banana (about 60 grams)
- 1 teaspoon of peanut (sugar-free from 100% peanuts)
- ½ teaspoon of chili sauce or a few drops of Tabasco

For decoration:

- almond slices, chili flakes

Seasoning:

- Salt and pepper, garlic powder if necessary

Preparation:

1. Place the pan on the stove and heat. If the pan is not anti-stick, put some frying oil into the pan of your choice.
2. Make a ball of minced meat and squeeze it flat between two layers of baking paper or foil. I always take the foil in which the butcher has packed the meat for me.
3. Season the meat with salt and pepper from both sides, put it immediately in the hot pan. Garlic powder or garlic pepper is also delicious.
4. While the meat is frying on the first side, decorate the salad as desired and slice the banana.
5. Turn the meat as soon as it is browned and fry the second side.
6. Add chili sauce to taste under peanut sauce.
7. Once the meat is cooked to your liking, put it on the lettuce bed, add the peanut cream, and decorate the bananas as a topping. Almond flakes and chili flakes over it, and off you go with the feast.

Recipe idea for the grill

Preparation on the grill is, of course, especially delicious! I would probably put the burger Patty in an aluminum package after the sharp grilling. On top of everything, sprinkle a small spoonful of honey or coconut sugar over it to caramelize.

In addition, a few glazed onions. This is the perfect burger recipe for the next BBQ party, where all bring their ultimate burger recipes.

37. Baked sweet potato with mozzarella and tomatoes

Ingredients

For 1 - 2 people (or depending on stomach size)

- 1 mozzarella (fat level of your choice) If you want very few calories, take Skyrella, which is very strong! For me, it does not work because of the minimizer ring!
- 1 medium tomato or several smaller tomatoes
- Basil leaves, freshly plucked
- 120 grams of sweet potato (adjust quantity as needed)
- A splash of olive oil
- Coarse salt, dried or fresh Italian herbs, garlic powder or fresh garlic.

Preparation:

1. Preheat the oven to 190 °C, place baking paper on the baking tray, and prepare. Add mozzarella/skyrella to the strainer to drain off the liquid.
2. Peel the sweet potato and cut into fried potatoes. The thinner they are, the faster they are cooked in the oven and crispy.
3. Massage sweet potatoes with a little olive oil. You can also paint them, but then you need more oil—and too much oil does not make them that crunchy. I, therefore, recommend using your hands.
4. Put sweet potatoes on the plate and sprinkle with the mixture of salt, herbs, and garlic. Do you use fresh herbs? Then please give it only for the last 5 minutes in the oven, which I find even more aromatic. Fresh herbs are a pleasure and do not want to be overheated. From the oven and every 5 minutes, see if the sweet potatoes have the right tan. The darker, the crisper. My potatoes took 14 minutes to reach the perfect point. It depends on the thickness of the discs and your preference.
5. Slice the mozzarella and tomatoes and decorate to taste on the plate. Leave room for the sweet potatoes.
6. If desired, you can drizzle mozzarella and tomatoes with high-quality olive oil. I love the raw enjoyment of a fair-made oil from Kalamata olives because it brings a typical

spicy taste of olive. I would never fry that, way too valuable and expensive. A pinch of Fleur de Sel or salt of your choice and the basil leaves, please only add directly before serving. Fresh black pepper is also very good if you like it a little spicier.

7. Once the sweet potatoes are ready, put them on the plate with tomato and mozzarella, and a quick lunch is finished with little work.

38. Potato wedges with herb quark "New York Bagel" Style

Potatoes and cottage cheese provide high-quality protein and are a good choice for a meal after a workout. But unfortunately, boring. Or isn't it?

With some bagel spices, I pimped the potatoes and mixed instead of normal quark, a delicious herb cottage cheese from yogurt, cottage cheese, and herbs.

This simple and quick dish tastes so good.

The hearty main course of a proven combination: potatoes and cottage cheese—put together with a dash. Portion is calculated to a total of about 150 grams because that's my "feel good." Of course, you can eat more or less of it!

INGREDIENTS

For the potato wedges

- 200 grams of raw potatoes with shell, washed
- 10 ml of olive oil
- 10 grams of sesame
- 10 grams of black cumin
- 10 grams of garlic, dried
- 3 grams of salt

For the herbal cottage cheese

- 200 grams of creamy cream cheese 0.8% fat
- 100 grams of Greek yogurt (2% fat)
- 40 grams of onions, finely diced
- 10 grams of Italian herbs TK or fresh
- Salt to taste
- Black pepper to taste
- Potato wedges protein quark recipe feature

Preparation

1. Potato wedges
2. Preheat oven cover baking tray with baking paper
3. Cut the potatoes into bite-sized pieces and place on the baking tray
4. Sprinkle olive oil over the potatoes and spread everything well with your hands; the potatoes should all be a little bit off.

5. Season with sesame, black cumin, and salt and bake in the oven for 25 minutes.

Herb quark

- All ingredients are only mixed together. There is nothing magical here. A fork is enough, so blender and co. may remain in the closet.

39. HIGH PROTEIN CREAMED VEGETABLES

Rich in protein and delicious, the casserole in tomato cream sauce shines with decent nutritional value. Add a turkey ball or some feta cheese on top, and the protein-rich meal is available.

Ingredients

- 100 grams of zucchini, finely diced
- 40 grams of red pepper, finely diced
- 30 grams of paprika, green, finely diced
- 1 tablespoon tomato paste
- ½ onion, finely chopped
- 1 teaspoon of brewing powder to taste
- 100 grams cream cheese half-fat or yogurt
- 60 milliliters of water
- 20 grams of collagen protein powder (e.g., allin Pure, Adozan, Primal Collagen)
- Creamy stomach bypass feature 1

Preparation

1. Cook the peppers softly in the pan for five minutes, then add the zucchini and cook for another 3 minutes. If you work without oil, you can add 2 tablespoons of water for a better frying result. It evaporates completely and helps to cook the vegetables.
2. Place the vegetables from the pan on a small plate.

3. In the pan, onions are then sweated with tomato paste until the onions are glassy and slightly fragrant.
4. Add the boil powder and the water, let the tomato sauce steeply boil.
5. Now the cream cheese has its appearance. Just put it in and combine it with the tomato sauce while stirring. Do not cook too much! At the very end, stir in the collagen protein powder, lift the vegetables into the sauce, and you're done.
6. Now there are no limits to your imagination: you can add fried strips of meat or salmon, serve meatballs, or just beat the stew with feta cheese or mozzarella.

40. Low carb French toast with cinnamon and bacon

Low carbohydrate French toast variation from tasty potato toastics.

Ingredients

Bread and bacon

- 1 potato toastie (or low carb rolls etc.)

For the egg mixture

- 1 pinch of cinnamon
- 1 egg
- 1 teaspoon vanilla powder erythrit or sweet of your choice
- 1 pinch of salt

Toppings

- 2 slices of bacon
- 3 raspberries (or more)
- 1 teaspoon sugar-free, low carb maple syrup

Preparation

1. Cut toastie into thin slices. Depending on the baking pan used, 2-4 slices are ideal.
2. Make the egg mixture by whisking the egg with the sweetness, salt, and cinnamon.
3. Put the toasties in the egg mixture. In the evening you should prepare everything, and let the toasts swell overnight. Otherwise, you should plan for about an hour of waiting, so that the low carb cake can properly soak with the egg mixture.
4. Put the pan on the stove and the bacon in the cold! Turn on the stove. The bacon fat may leak better, and you do not need to eat it (unless you want to, that's ok!). The bacon is ready when it is lightly browned. Place it on the kitchen stairs to absorb excess grease.
5. If you want to fry without fat—no problem with a well-coated pan—wipe the rest of the bacon fat with a kitchen crepe out of the pan before frying the soaked toasties in golden yellow on both sides. I fry the mid-range of my hearth (4 out of 9).
6. Finally, pour the bacon into the pan again, so that it gets nice and warm. Decorate the plate with fruit, if you like.
7. Depending on your preference, you can eat sugar-free or normal maple syrup, powdered erythrit, home-made "healthy Nutella," or a topping of your choice.

41. Protein pizza dough for low carb pizza

A simple protein-rich pizza dough without special ingredients is a great way to treat yourself to a pizza and, at the same time, get your protein. The presented pizza delivers just under 28 grams of protein and weighs 194 grams.

How much you can eat is individual! It's okay to eat pizza completely. Just pay attention to your saturation.

High-protein pizza dough made from three simple ingredients, delicious with chicken breast, green asparagus, paprika, and cheese.

INGREDIENTS

For the pizza dough

- 2 egg whites (or 1 egg whole)
- 40 grams of grated cheese (light)
- 15 grams of quark, lean

- 1 level teaspoon of pizza spice
- 10 grams of chopped onions (optional)

For the tomato sauce

- 1 tablespoon tomato paste
- 1 teaspoon Italian herbs (TK or fresh)
- 1 teaspoon of Erythrit (or other Low-carb sweetness)

For covering:

- 15 grams of chicken breast cut extremely fine cut
- 15 grams of paprika, finely diced red
- 1 stick of asparagus, finely chopped green
- 10 grams of grated cheese

Preparation

1. Preheat oven to 180 degrees circulating air/200 degrees upper/lower heat. Pizza form provisions - when preparing pizza-style, I would provide a large plate with cut baking paper and the dough there on it.
2. Place all ingredients for the dough in a blender or Magic Bullet/Moulinette purée to dough together.
3. Put the dough on a small pizza pan.
4. Leave pizzateig 15 minutes in the oven until it is well browned but not too dark.

5. In the meantime, cut the ingredients for the topping very finely and stir together the ingredients for the tomato sauce.
6. Now the dough will spread like a normal pizza with the tomato sauce, topping it, sprinkle with cheese and sprinkle pizza seasoning on it again.
7. Serve hot or cold! The pizza also tastes good the next day, if some is left over. It's also great to eat at work or school.

42. Extra Soft Scrambled Egg

This extra-soft scrambled egg is the variant that I best tolerate. It is a very simple recipe; it depends mainly on the preparation.

Ingredients

- 2 eggs
- 30 grams of Greek yogurt (2% fat)
- 1 pinch of vegetable broth or chicken broth powder

Preparation

1. Place a non-stick pan on the stove and set on low heat. For me, I set to level 4 (of 9).
2. Mix the egg with the vegetable stock and the yogurt. The Greek yogurt with 2% fat is best suited for this. It is creamy and more like sour cream in consistency but not so greasy.
3. When the pan is preheated, add the egg mixture. Now it depends on your patience. The egg should cook only very slowly. You

gently push it in "clods" through the pan until it gets a little firmer. The surface should still shine and look slightly "raw." No wild "stirring!"

4. As soon as it looks good, pull the pan off the stove and set it aside. You can now either prepare vegetables or a small side dish, cover a table or similar. After about 5 minutes, the egg should "pull."

5. Decorate the finished portion nicely, possibly salting to taste. While roasting, there may not be too much salt in the egg mass, which otherwise dries!

43. Glycine in the diet and pork sausage

Ingredients:

- 1 kg rinds, cooked, chopped
- 1 large onion, cooked with the rinds and minced
- 800g of minced meat (a mixture of your choice, I have 50% rather low-fat meat and 50% fat-rich meat)
- Allspice
- Pepper
- Ursala
- Mustard seeds

Preparation:

Prepare a sufficient quantity of preserving glasses (sterilize, including the lid, check all parts for integrity); if necessary, boil the filling aid and tools (cooking tweezers, cooking spoons, etc.).

Preparation of cooked pan sausage (sorrel):

Mix minced meat and cracked rind-onion mixture well and season with the spices. The easiest way is in the food processor; the "dough" can be kneaded so that everything mixes well. The finished mass is then filled in preserving jars; it should remain free to the upper edge about 2-3 cm. This is important for later cooking! Close the glasses—being careful not to touch the edge of the glass or the inside of the lid with your hands or unsterilized tool. You should pay attention during filling, not to "dirty" the edge of the glass with the dough; the boiling process succeeds better if the sausage was filled clean.

Place the filled and closed jars in the drip pan or casserole dish and then add enough water to the dripping pan so that the jars are about 2 cm deep in the water.

Then set the oven to 180 degrees, and as soon as the liquid begins to boil in the glasses, continue cooking for another half hour or so.

Next, lower the temperature in the oven to 150 degrees and cook for another 90 minutes.

After 90 minutes, the glasses should remain in the oven for at least half an hour before they can be removed for cooling. I just leave the glasses in the oven and take them out when they're cold.

Check the ready-cooked glasses for a successful cooking process. the lids must be tightly closed—with my glasses I recognize this by the fact that the lid has sucked a little bit inwards from the negative pressure in the glass (which is caused by cooking, and therefore it is important that the glass is not filled too much).

Glasses that are not properly cooked should be checked for damage to glass or (more often) lids. If everything seems to be okay, you can either reheat or cook as described above, if it is a single glass, I would just put it in the fridge and consume within the next 2-3 weeks. The cooked glasses are best kept cool and dark at the same temperature in the basement or a storeroom. If the basement is not dark, you can wrap aluminum foil around the glasses,

Preparing a meal with the pan sausage

The best thing about the pan sausage is its durability. If it is properly cooked, you can have it well uncooled in the basement. That's why I made a big batch right away. If you do not have much time left, you can get a glass from the cellar, and you have it ready in a few minutes.

1. Remove the settled fat from the jar and put it in the pan.
2. Cut an onion into small pieces and sweat in fat until they are glassy or golden brown to taste (I prefer golden brown).
3. Add the pan sausage to the onions in the pan (medium heat is enough) and crush them into pieces. The pan sausage begins very quickly to "melt" because the rinds are not noticeable as rinds per se; they also have no great taste. If the sausage is well seasoned, you do not need to spice anything up. The boiling process needs some seasoning because the spices get weaker when boiled, and thus, sometimes too little seasoning is in it—so, taste from the sausage pan. You can even brown them on

request in a non-stick pan—I just made them nice and hot and creamy.

In Lower Saxony, you can eat traditional jacket potatoes—I've combined them with butternut pumpkin from the oven and tomato salad. Sure, it's home cooking, but who says you cannot experiment with it? I have already made the Bolognese variant, just some tomato paste, and a can of lumpy tomatoes stirred under the little wings, and there's the special Zucchini noodle sauce, which at the same time beats the glycine dilemma.

By the way, a sweet potato, which I had filled with the pan sausage and baked with some hard cheese, came out really well. Very hearty, somehow untraditional, and made fast.

Have a good appetite, and enjoy cooking.

Protein Cake & Sweet Pastries

44. Quark Keulchen Lower Carb

Ingredients

Ingredients for 4 - 5 small curd cubes (about 1 - 2 servings, depending on how long ago you have undergone surgery)

- 160 grams of skimmed quark
- 1 egg
- 20 grams of spelled flour
- 10 grams of whey isolate
- 1 pinch of salt
- 1 pinch of baking powder As
- desired Erythrit, Flav Drops o.Ä. for sweetening

Preparation:

1. In the Mini Blender (e.g., Magic Bullet) or with the blender, mix all ingredients to a thick paste and put aside for a short time.
2. Place the pan over medium heat and let it heat up. With very good adhesion,

additional coating fat is unnecessary, otherwise use fat for the pan.

3. Once the pan is evenly hot, add small "heaps" to the pan, one tablespoon at a time. I like to paint them around so that they look like pancakes—but that's just a quirk. The form does not matter.

4. Once you've spread the dough, lower the pan to low heat and let the curd cheese fry untouched until you discover small bubbles on the top edge.

5. Now you can turn the curds carefully— but please do not! Due to the reduced amount of flour, the babies are slightly more sensitive than normal Quark chew. Therefore, they should bake well in low heat before you turn them.

6. Fry the curds and serve them warm with, for example, powdered Erythrit and fresh fruit or a teaspoon of hazelnut sauce. Applesauce, creamy Greek yogurt with 2% fat as "cream sauce" and strawberries are also very good. Your imagination knows no boundaries.

45. Protein Cheesecake Muffins

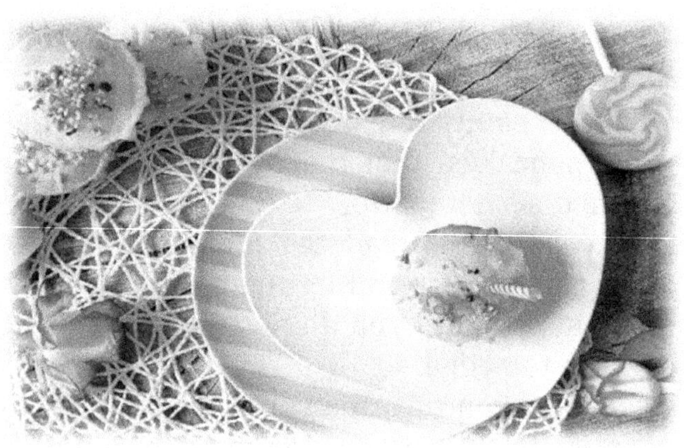

Ingredients

- 250 grams of quark (20% fat)
- 1 tablespoon of coconut oil, melted (about 10 grams)
- 2 eggs
- 1 tablespoon of lemon juice
- 1 pinch of lemon zest
- 1 pinch of salt
- 1 heaped tablespoon of wheat semolina
- 30 grams of vanilla whey isolate (I recommend Gym Prior food-spring)
- 1 tablespoon vanilla Erythrit
- 1 teaspoon baking soda

Of course, you can also bake with curd cheese. The muffins will then become drier. If you want very sweet cupcakes, the dough needs more sweetness. For a "normally sweet" quark dough, for example, you should add about 30 grams of Erythrit or a few drops of Flavor Drops.

Preparation

1. Preheat the oven to 160 degrees. Provide a muffin mold (12er). If you are not using a silicone mold, grease the baking pan.
2. Mix all wet ingredients first to a smooth mass and let them frothy for about 3-5 minutes. This is not necessary, it only makes the cheesecake muffins looser and fluffier.
3. Now add the dry ingredients gradually to the cheese mass until everything is beautifully mixed evenly.
4. Divide the cheese mass into 12 muffin cases. For decoration, you can sprinkle with almonds or hazelnuts. Surely you can also add fruit. Just be intuitive and follow your appetite.
5. On the bottom shelf of my oven, I baked the muffins for 32 minutes at 160 degrees Celsius. Then I turned off the oven and opened the door a crack.
6. Give the cheesecake muffins time to cool slowly. After a quarter of an hour, you can open the oven door completely, and after half an hour, you bring it out.
7. Are you in a hurry and want to start eating without waiting? Always start with the muffins; they only fall a little stronger when they cool down quickly.

46. Protein Madeleines With Apricot And Chocolate

Ingredients

Returns 18 pieces/3 sheets

- 165 grams of the egg (whole egg)
- 125 grams skyr, natural or vanilla (vanilla skyr from Lidl has the least amount of sugar)
- 50 ml of milk
- 20 grams of almond flour
- 15 grams of coconut flour
- 20 Grams Whey Isolate (Cookies and Cream or Vanilla)
- 1 teaspoon of psyllium husk
- 60 grams apricots, small diced (fresh). Dried fruit is safe, but has more sugar.
- 1 packet of orange peel (e.g., Alnatura) or orange grated
- 30 grams of chocolate drops, sugar-free
- 1 teaspoon of baking powder
- A little vanilla and a pinch of salt

Preparing

1. Preheat the oven to 160 degrees; turn out Madeleine's mold.
2. If you do not take the high-quality silicone baking pan, please grease your shape well. The dough otherwise sticks tightly.
3. Mix moist ingredients in a bowl.

4. In a separate bowl, mix dry ingredients well, except for drops of chocolate and apricots.
5. Add dry ingredients to the moist ingredients in tablespoons. Lastly, fold in the chocolate drops and the apricot cubes with a wooden spoon.
6. Spread the dough into the molds and allow for swelling for 5 minutes, then place in the oven.
7. Depending on the desired degree of browning and oven, the Madeleines are ready after 12-15 minutes. Traditionally, they are relatively light, because even here, the pastry tastes much better when it is heated slightly before consumption (e.g., on the bread holder of the toaster).

47. Low-carb Biscuit

These peanut cookies are low in carbohydrates, high in protein, and damn delicious—but they are mainly made from peanuts. For the slimline, these cookies are only suitable if they fit into the nutritional plan. 2 - 3 of these biscuits replace a full meal, they are not "snacks," although I basically do not recommend unplanned "snoozing" anyway. A single cookie has just over 9 grams of protein!

Now that the unromantic details are clear, let's go to the ingredients. By the way: if you want to make the recipe "paleo," just substitute the peanut with almond paste or some other nutmeg, and you have biscuits free from legumes. (Peanuts are legumes and contain many lectins).

Ingredients

(12 cookies)

- 125 g peanut butter (peanut butter without any additives, purely from the nuts)

- 70 grams of almond flour, partially oiled or ground almonds (making it juicier)
- 40 Grams Premium Whey Isolate (Peanut Butter Cookie Flavor or Cookies & Cream are Perfect). Attention - often sold out because of the great demand, every now and then look again.
- 30 Gramm Erythrit
- 1 teaspoon vanilla cream or vanilla erythritol
- 15 grams of organic coconut oil
- 3 grams of blood pressure salt or another salt

I use the Premium Isolate because it is super fine and can be incorporated better in the biscuits. You can take any other protein, too; it just does not make such a tender crunch. In these cookies, salt is necessary! I prefer potassium salt (blood pressure salt), but you can take any salt.

Preparation:

1. Preheat the oven to 190 degrees, layout the baking sheet with parchment paper.
2. Knead all ingredients into a dough in the food processor or with the hand mixer.
3. Use your hands to shape 12 balls out of the dough and place them on the baking tray.
4. Flatten the biscuit with a fork and immortalize the typical American peanut butter cookie pattern.

The problem with storage of peanut butter protein biscuits

"Theoretical," at least, because these biscuits have many natural predators. If I were you, I would hide them from anyone else—or live with them vanishing in a hurry. And no: The double recipe to bake, also uses nothing. Somehow the crispy biscuits disappear just as fast as magic. So here's the warning: beware, they are addictive—even for people who are not necessarily low carb fetishists.

48. Birthday Cake Slices

Ingredients

- Birthday Cake Protein Powder
- Ground almonds instead of raw cocoa powder
- If you do not have a great birthday cake protein, that's not bad. The Taste Birthday cake is a vanilla biscuit with a delicate lemon note and colorful sprinkles. You can, for example, just work with vanilla protein, e.g., Zero light in Vanilla Ice, and add some lemon flavor.

Changed ingredients for the cream:

- Again, you can exchange the protein with the Birthday Cake and add some grated lemon peel to the cream. Easy.

- Maybe you need some colorful sprinkles. I have enough only for the decoration. Their taste to me is not 100% ideal.

Preparation

The rest of the preparation is just like milk cuts.

Note on baking:

This dough is delicate. It should have at most a slight tan, but best kept bright. It dries out easily due to the low fat.

49. Hazelnut Chocolate Donut

Ingredients:

For the dough: (12 pieces)

- 165 grams of egg
- 125 grams of protein quark, skinny quark or skyr
- 100 grams of ground hazelnuts (or almonds)
- 75 ml of milk
- 60 grams Whey Isolate Cookies & Cream or Vanilla
- 15 grams of psyllium husk
- 20 grams of melted coconut oil or melted butter
- 1 teaspoon of baking powder
- 3 drops of butter vanilla flavor

For the glaze:

- 100 grams of low carb chocolate, melted
- 50 grams of chopped hazelnuts

Preparation:

1. Preheat oven to 160 degrees, provide silicone mold.
2. Process the dough in a large bowl with the kitchen blender or in the food processor to a smooth batter. Just add all the ingredients at once! Yes, it's that easy.

3. Put in the donut molds with the dough and then put in the oven for 20 - 15 minutes. Please do the chopstick test on the first baking!
4. Let the donuts cool in the mold for 10 minutes. Otherwise, the dough is too soft and goes badly out of shape.
5. After 10 minutes, let the donuts cool completely on a grate.

The protein donuts taste great even without glaze. They are juicy, and I think you do not need a glaze. Still, I did one for the eye. Simply melt 100 grams of low carb chocolate of your choice and dunk the donuts into the liquid chocolate. Sprinkle the protein donuts with chopped hazelnuts for a beautiful look.

You can pick up the donuts in an airtight Tupperware container for a few days in the fridge if there are no natural predators (such as hungry husbands, etc.). Otherwise, they can actually freeze even with the glaze. That surprised me but worked great. Simply freeze each side by side in the freezer bag and take out two hours before consumption and allow to thaw at room temperature.

With glaze and hazelnut decoration (glaze 50/50 from drops of sugar and chocolate whole milk & dark bitter)

- Per piece (60 grams)
- 188 calories

- 14 grams of fat (4g saturated)
- 4 grams of carbohydrates
- 1 gram of fiber
- 11 grams of protein

Protein donut compared to a normal donut from the baker with glaze:

Standard donut with cocoa-based glaze

- 60 grams serving
- 253 calories
- 14.7 grams of fat
- 25.3 grams of carbohydrates
- 4.1 grams of protein

50. Strawberry cheesecake protein cake

Ingredients

- 1 piece of protein cake/breakfast cake
- 1 tablespoon of Greek yogurt 0.2%
- 1 tablespoon cream cheese, reduced-fat or optional (I took Buko Skyr)
- 1 drop of Cheesecake Flavor or simply sweet of your choice
- 1 tablespoon of lemon juice
- 2 strawberries (or as many as you want on it)
- 1 Amaretti (1 gram)

Preparation

- Place protein cake on a plate.
- Mix yogurt, cream cheese, flavor drops, and lemon juice to a smooth mass and pour on the protein cake. Serve with strawberries and a crushed amaretti.

51. Protein Yogurt Waffles With Ice Cream

Waffle Recipe Variant for a baking mix for waffles and pancakes. Instead of butter and milk, there is Greek yogurt (2% fat) and a portion of extra protein from protein powder. The waffles are nice and soft and taste delicious.

Ingredients

For the waffle dough

- 20 grams of Dr. Almond waffle mix
- 10 grams of whey protein powder or collagen (e.g., Zero light, allin Pure, Adozan)
- 80 grams of Greek yogurt (2% fat)
- 1 egg (size L)
- 3 drops of FlavDrops taste lard cake
- ¼ pod of vanilla (or vanilla Zucker)
- 1 pinch of salt
- 1 pinch of cinnamon

For the topping

- 2 scoops of low-calorie ice
- 2 teaspoons of hazelnut sauce roasted

Preparation

1. Preheat the waffle iron and grease if necessary (my iron does not need any fat.) The dough is relatively low in fat and could be put in a brand new iron or in a bad adhesive coating!
2. Pu all ingredients for the dough in a blender/small blender and purée shortly. Alternatively, of course, the preparation can be done with a stirring spoon.
3. Add half of the dough to the preheated iron and bake the waffle until golden brown. With my iron, I set the heat to low, and baking takes about one and a half minutes.
4. Put the finished waffle on a plate and serve with an ice cream ball and a little hazelnut sauce.
5. Tip: If you want to pick up the second waffle, you can even freeze it! It can then be thawed in the microwave for a few seconds or pushed into the toaster to bake.

52. Protein milk cuts (low-fat, low-carb)

A delicious low-calorie protein-rich variant of the milk cuts can also be good as a snack at work or to take to school.

Ingredients

For the dough

- 5 eggs Gr. M
- 100 milliliters of mineral water
- 60 grams of almond flour partially oiled
- 40 grams of chocolate protein powder (whey)
- 15 grams of psyllium husk
- 15 grams of baking cocoa
- 40 grams of inulin (soluble fiber, light sweetness)
- 1 pod of vanilla, scratched out
- ½ sachet of baking powder
- 1 pinch of natron

For the filling

- 2 packs of instant gelatin
- 1 egg white beaten stiff
- 180 grams of cream cheese (fat level of your choice, I use 4%)
- 100 milliliters of milk
- 30 grams of protein powder "honey & milk" flavor (or your personal choice)
- 2-3 drops of orange flavor (or abrasion)

Preparations

1. Preheat oven to 180 degrees. Prepare a baking tray with baking paper.

This is how you make the dough:

2. Mix all dry ingredients in a bowl, set aside for a moment.
3. Beat the eggs with the mineral water in the food processor for a few minutes until frothy. Then add the dry ingredients by tablespoons. The result is a creamy, brown dough that tastes raw and good. Tip: Taste it. If the sweetness is not enough for you, you can improve to taste.
4. Spread the dough on a baking tray. With a dough spatula, you can get a very thin dough for more milk cuts—I prefer the dough thicker and nicely juicy.
5. The dough now wanders about 14 minutes in the oven, do the stick test if in doubt.

Afterward, you should, after a very short cooling phase, carefully remove the baking paper so that the dough does not "sweat." Allow the dough plate to cool completely.

6. If necessary, smooth the edges of the floor.
7. Split the cooled plate into two halves, which you can then fold over each other like a sandwich. The two halves should be about the same size.
8. When the plates are prepared, it is time to prepare the filling.

Preparation of protein filling:

9. First, whip the egg whites stiff in the food processor and set it aside.
10. Stir the cream cheese with the milk and add the remaining ingredients. The easiest way is also in the food processor. Finally, pour the instant gelatin into the mass.
11. In the smooth cream, carefully lift the egg whites with a wooden spoon. The egg whites serve as a "substitute" for the cream that is used in many recipes.

Mount milk cuts

1. Spread the protein-rich cream evenly on one of the two dough plates, smooth everything smoothly, and place the other plate on top as a lid.
2. The protein milk cuts should stay at least 4 hours in the refrigerator so that the gelatin

firms with the cream. I recommend having the milk cuts pulled for 8 hours or more. The dough then absorbs a little liquid and, at the same time, becomes drier from the outside. So it's great to prepare the day before!

3. Well chilled, cut the milk slices now in portion-appropriate bits. Be sure to follow your stomach size. For me, 60 grams "fits" best.

4. I froze the milk slices in a Tupper box. In the fridge, they slowly thawed overnight and were great again! So you can freeze some.